Best Bites
From The
Wellness Kitchen

**Experience the Joy of
Cooking Healthy Recipes**

OSU ▲ SERETEAN WELLNESS CENTER
OKLAHOMA STATE UNIVERSITY

"Real Solutions for Real People"

OSU **SERETEAN WELLNESS CENTER**
OKLAHOMA STATE UNIVERSITY

Helping people achieve a balance of physical and mental health.

The concept behind *Best Bites* was a simple one…encouraging consumers to buy the freshest foods available and teaching them how to prepare delicious meals that are lower in fat, sodium and cholesterol.

Proceeds from the sale of the cookbook will be used to fund wellness programs at Oklahoma State University. It is part of the University's long-term goal of making the Stillwater campus among the healthiest in the Nation.

Additional copies of *Best Bites* are available for $19.95 plus applicable taxes and shipping charges. To order these copies, phone 405.744-WELL or log on to our website at www.wellness.okstate.edu.

First Printing   September, 2005

ISBN: 0-9768634-0-5

Seretean Wellness Center
Oklahoma State University
1514 West Hall of Fame
Stillwater, OK 74078-2026

WIMMER
COOKBOOKS

A CONSOLIDATED GRAPHICS COMPANY

800.548.2537   wimmerco.com

Introduction

The Seretean Wellness Center opened in January 1991, named after its major benefactor and proponent Dr. M.B. "Bud" Seretean. Dr. Seretean champions wellness and embodies it in every aspect of his life. His belief and commitment to nutrition as an essential part of wellness programming resulted in a demonstration kitchen being included in the Center's building plans.

What has become a consistent feature of the Seretean Wellness Center—the cooking classes—has led to the publication of this book. The concept behind the classes seemed simple enough: buy the freshest foods available and teach people how to prepare delicious meals that are lower in fat, sodium, and cholesterol. With ready-prepared foods and fast food available everywhere, the initial challenge would be convincing attendees that cooking is neither a chore nor a difficult skill to learn. To appeal to a wide range of cooking abilities and personal tastes, many recipes would also have to be easy to prepare; some would also take more time. Fortunately, our location on a university campus offered ready opportunities to feature international and regional cuisines. From Chinese stir-fry to Southern pulled pork, the recipes in this book reflect that diversity.

Of course, without the interest and help of guest instructors and chefs, this cookbook would not be possible. Each semester a new series of cooking classes would begin, sometimes with instructors who love to cook but who have had no official culinary training, other times with individuals who have degrees from cooking schools and have owned restaurants. All helped the cause.

Since joining the Wellness Center staff in 1991, I have been fortunate to meet and work with many individuals who share a genuine interest in nutrition and health. As a registered dietitian and former owner of a food business, there is gratification in seeing the result of fifteen years of classes with the support of all the staff at the center become this cookbook. May all of you who have provided feedback and taken the time to test its many recipes enjoy what you have created.

~Elizabeth Lohrman

Vegetable Cooking Tips

Steaming—Since steaming vegetables retains the greatest amount of their flavor and nutritional value, it is clearly a preferred method. Greens like spinach and chard are wonderful lightly steamed, but they cook very quickly, so a rule of thumb for tender greens is to place them in a boiling steamer, cover them, and count to "8 hippopotamus's." Tender greens also usually "cook down" by half, thus always use your largest stock pot, a steamer (one that has little feet that rest in the bottom of the pot and open up to a flat basket) or a steamer insert. Fill the pot with water right below the bottom of the basket and let it come to a rapid boil. Fill up the pot with as much green as you can fit. For heartier vegetables like broccoli, use the fork method (i.e., pierce them with a fork to see if they are tender) and add a little more water if needed.

Sautéing—While commonly used to prepare other foods, sautéing, hot, rapid cooking using an oil or fat, is a great way to prepare vegetables. A light olive oil and fresh vegetables will produce the best results. Sauté broccoli with freshly sliced garlic and become a believer in this method's possibilities.

Searing—Searing is one cooking method that is rarely used with vegetables. If you have never had sliced cauliflower seared and drizzled with olive oil and then topped with a squeeze of lemon, you don't know what you are missing! Searing uses the same techniques as sautéing, but it takes a little more time to brown vegetables, like pancakes, on each side. You can sear most hearty vegetables like cabbage, cauliflower, broccoli, parsnip, rutabaga, turnip, and carrot. Lightly season them with pepper, or your favorite herb, and enjoy.

Roasting—Many have not experienced the wonderful taste of roasted root vegetables. This method brings out the natural sugars present in beets, parsnips, rutabagas, turnips, potatoes, yams, and whole cloves of garlic. The preparation is simple. Cut the vegetables into large cubes or wedges of the same size and toss them in a little olive oil, just enough to lightly coat. Then spread them out evenly on a baking sheet and roast on the top rack of a 400° oven for approximately 40 minutes or until lightly browned. Cauliflower and broccoli are especially tasty when prepared this way.

Storing vegetables—Remember that once a vegetable is picked, it begins to lose its nutrient values. So fresh is best when it comes to veggies! As great as they are, refrigerators dehydrate food, and so when it comes to storing vegetables, always cut the greens off vegetables like carrots, beets, kohlrabi, turnips and radishes. Since the greens continue to seek moisture from the root, they encourage more dehydration. Don't forget, however, that the greens from these veggies are great steamed or sautéed, so don't throw them away. Most vegetables can be stored in refrigerators, but there are notable exceptions such as tomatoes, garlic, and onions. The texture and flavor of these three vegetables are negatively affected by refrigeration and will actually last longer if they are kept at room temperature.

A common problem when it comes to vegetables is quantity. It can be more difficult to cook for two people than for twenty because many vegetables are usually available in a bunch or head. How can one or two people eat a bunch of celery before it goes south? The obvious first step is to use the celery as you typically would: cut up one or two ribs and put them in a soup or a potato salad. Wrap the rest in foil and store it in the refrigerator. It will last for several weeks or longer in perfect condition. Since lettuce can also spoil quickly, you can prevent waste by cutting it, cleaning it, and drying it in a salad spinner; then store it in plastic bags. You will have lettuce ready to go every night for the whole week.

Vegetable soups—Soups are an easy way to add more vegetables to your diet. Even picky-eaters will usually not turn down a creamy asparagus soup or one made with fresh butternut squash.

Meat Cookery

Sautéing:

Sautéing is a dry-heat cooking method using some type of fat such as olive oil or butter, and thin, small (portion-sized), high-quality cuts of meat. Chicken breasts, turkey cutlets, certain cuts of beef or pork, and fillets of fish will cook in less time. To prevent uneven cooking, use a meat mallet to pound meat out to a similar thickness throughout.

To prevent meat from sticking, heat your pan (preferably one with short, sloped sides) over medium-high heat. Wash and dry the meat and season to taste with salt and pepper. When the pan is hot, add oil or butter and then the meat. Do not crowd items in the pan; adequate space allows food to brown rather than steam. Before turning the meat, let the pan come back to medium-high heat. A small item should not take more than several minutes per side to cook, although everyone will decide when something is "done." Color is also an important factor to consider; cook most meat to a golden brown. To test if meat is done, press it with your finger; it should be firm to the touch.

Sautéing is usually completed on the stovetop, but meat can be browned quickly and then finished in the oven at about 400°. This technique works well for thicker pieces of meat or chicken rather than thinner cuts.

Grilling:

Grilling is a cooking technique for tender cuts of high-quality beef, pork, chicken, or fish (two inches thick at most). You can grill on an electric, propane, charcoal, or hardwood grill or stovetop grill pan. To prepare the grill, clean it and lightly oil the grill rack. Make sure the grill is hot before adding the meat. For added flavor, marinate the meat beforehand. Grill thinner cuts of meat at high heat as quickly as possible on both sides. Start thicker cuts on high heat then turn and move them to a cooler area of the grill to finish. If you wish to prevent the exterior of thicker cuts of meat from burning, transfer it to an oven-proof pan and finish it in a hot oven (400°). Foods should be grilled at the last minute—a few minutes per side for rare or up to 8 minutes per side for well done, depending on the thickness.

Roasting:

Roasting is a dry-heat cooking method done in the oven, similar to baking. Oven temperatures generally range from 250° to 425°, depending upon the size and tenderness of the meat. Roast tougher cuts such as chuck or rump roasts at a lower temperature and expect larger, tender cuts of meat (chicken, turkeys, and pork or beef roasts) to take longer to cook. Pre-preparation may involve stuffing, boning, tying, or seasoning. Tying a roast evens the shape, assists in proper carving, and improves heat distribution. A smaller roast should be browned first on the stovetop then roasted in the oven to the desired internal temperature. Doing so will enhance flavor and color. Use a pan that is open, low-sided, and suitable for the size of meat. Add a rack to the pan to elevate the meat from the juices and for even browning.

Do not pierce a roast as it is cooking because it can lose moisture if punctured. During the roasting process, baste lean cuts of meat with the juices. When a roast is 5° from the optimal internal temperature, remove it from the oven. It will continue cooking since the outside layer is warmer than the inside, and heat will be transferred to the middle (known as carryover cooking). Let the roast rest for at least 10 minutes before carving to allow the juices to disperse through the meat.

For an internal temperature of roasted meats, an instant-read thermometer is helpful:
  Beef: 145° for medium • Pork: 140° • Poultry: 160°

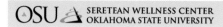

Table of Contents

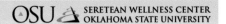
The Seretean Wellness Center thanks all the cooks who contributed their original recipes to this book. We regret that we were unable to include all the recipes. We hope that we have not inadvertently overlooked anyone. A special thanks to all the staff for taste-testing so many recipes over the past fifteen years, and to the students from the nutritional sciences department for helping with preparation and serving during the cooking classes.

Alan Adolphson

Bobby and Leah Aufill

Tom Baggot

Lisa Becklund

Pam Bettis

Ann Bingham

Elaine Dent

Jane Earnest

Homa Ghajar

Diane and Bob Graalman

Mike Gunzenhauser

Bill Harris

Shida Henneberry

Jerry Jackson

William Jaco

Nan Jones

Elizabeth Lohrman

Patricia Majid

Louise Martin

Susan Massaron

Mac McCrory

Nancy Mills

Carol Moder

Johanna Moretti

Robin Purdie

Sarah Ramsay

Gene Solomon

Jeremy Spector

Sally Walkiewicz

Joyce Zorba

Vegetable Cooking Tips
   by Chef Lisa Becklund

Meat Cookery by Chef Sarah Ramsay

Food Photography by Tammy Shaffer

Food Styling by Elizabeth Lohrman

Pottery made by Rebecca Livingston
   and Bill Minter

Copy Editor: Kendria Cost

Cover Design: Brad Cost

Asian Eggplant Dip

1	large eggplant (about 1 pound) pricked several times with a fork
1	clove garlic, minced
2	green onions, chopped
¼	cup cilantro, chopped
1	tablespoon fresh ginger, peeled and minced
2	teaspoons light soy sauce
2	teaspoons lemon juice
2	teaspoons sesame oil

Place eggplant on double thickness of paper towels and cook uncovered in microwave on high for 12 minutes.

When eggplant is cool enough to handle, cut it in half lengthwise and scoop out the flesh. Add garlic, green onions, cilantro, ginger, and soy sauce and process in food processor until mixture is coarsely chopped.

Transfer to serving bowl and stir in lemon juice and sesame oil. Serve with lightly toasted wedges of pita bread.

Yield: 2 cups; Serves: 6; Calories: 35; Protein: 0 g; Carbohydrate: 5 g;
Total fat: 1.5 g; Saturated fat: 0 g; Cholesterol: 0 g; Fiber: 2 g; Sodium: 115 mg

Black Bean, Corn, and Pepper Salsa

2	(14 ounce) cans black beans, rinsed and drained
1	(10 ounce) package frozen corn, barely cooked
1	small green pepper, diced
1	small red pepper, diced
2	garlic cloves, minced
3	tablespoons lime juice
1	jalapeño pepper, minced
1	ripe avocado, diced
¼	cup olive oil
1	fresh tomato, diced
½	cup fresh cilantro, finely chopped
	Salt and pepper to taste
	Tortilla chips

In large bowl, mix beans, corn, peppers, garlic, lime juice, jalapeño, avocado, and olive oil. Gently stir in tomato and cilantro. Season with salt and pepper if desired. Serve with chips for dipping.

Yield: 10 cups; Serving size: ½ cup; Calories: 80; Protein: 3 g; Carbohydrate: 10 g; Total fat: 3 g; Saturated fat: 0 g; Cholesterol: 0 mg; Fiber: 3 g; Sodium: 160 mg

*Purchase baked chips or chips made with liquid oil rather than hydrogenated oil. Check sodium content to choose a product with less salt.

Crispy Tofu Phyllo Triangles

2   **teaspoons olive oil**

½   **cup shredded carrots**

2   **tablespoons scallions, thinly sliced**

1   **teaspoon fresh ginger, peeled and minced**

2   **cloves garlic, minced**

3   **ounces firm tofu, finely cut**

     Salt to taste

4   **sheets phyllo**

     Olive oil for brushing

Filling:

In medium sauté pan over medium heat, cook carrots, scallions, ginger and garlic in olive oil for about 2 to 3 minutes. Add tofu and salt and cook another minute. Set aside while preparing phyllo.

To make the triangles:

Preheat oven to 375°. Line sheet pan with parchment paper. Let phyllo dough come to room temperature before using. Carefully unroll dough and remove 4 sheets. Tightly wrap remaining dough in plastic wrap. Lay one sheet out on work surface, with short side at the bottom. Cover remaining sheets with slightly damp cloth towel to prevent them from drying out.

Brush phyllo sheet with olive oil, covering completely, including all edges. Cut sheet into 3 equal size strips. Place 2 teaspoons of filling at the bottom of first strip and fold strip up like flag, not too tightly, ending up with small triangular packet. Brush top with olive oil and lay triangle on sheet pan. Continue with remaining phyllo and filling. If not baking right away, cover triangles with plastic wrap and refrigerate until ready to use. They also freeze well and can be baked right out of the freezer. Bake for 12 minutes or until golden brown. They are best served immediately. Serve with Firecracker Sauce, page 134.

Yield: 12 triangles; Calories: 45; Protein: 2 g; Carbohydrate: 4 g; Total fat: 2 g;
Saturated fat: 0 g; Cholesterol: 0 mg; Fiber: 0 g; Sodium: 35 mg

*Use tofu within three days of opening.
It can be added to soups or main dishes. Since it is mild in flavor,
using spices and marinade will enhance the taste.

Crostini with Roasted Peppers

3	large red bell peppers
2	tablespoons olive oil
1	large garlic clove, minced
2	teaspoons minced fresh rosemary leaves or ½ teaspoon dried (or substitute thyme)
12	slices toasted semolina bread (or any good quality Italian or sourdough bread)
⅓	cup Gorgonzola cheese, crumbled
¼	teaspoon fresh ground pepper

Rinse peppers under cold running water. Cut peppers in half, remove seeds (or leave peppers whole if using gas stove) and place under broiler until black and charred all over. Put peppers in brown paper bag and seal or in pan with a tight-fitting cover. Let peppers stand until cooled, about 20 minutes. The skin should separate easily from pepper. Quarter peppers and lay flat in glass dish. Combine olive oil, garlic and rosemary; spread mixture over peppers. Let stand 30 minutes to 1 hour.

Toast bread slices; next divide peppers evenly among bread slices. Top with crumbled cheese and fresh grind of pepper. Put crostini under broiler until cheese is bubbling, about 1 to 2 minutes. Watch closely so bread does not burn.

Serves: 6; Serving size: 2 toasts; Calories: 245; Protein: 8 g; Carbohydrate: 33 g;
Total fat: 9 g; Saturated fat: 2 g; Cholesterol: 5 mg; Fiber: 3 g; Sodium: 450 mg

To roast fresh chiles or bell peppers, try one of the following two methods:

1. Over a gas burner on the stove, spear chiles or peppers on a long handled fork, place over the flame, and heat until the skin is blistered and darkened all over.

2. Place chiles or peppers on baking sheet and broil in the oven until the skin is dark. Turn frequently to roast the entire chile.

Once roasted, place hot chiles or peppers in a plastic bag or airtight container and let steam. Once they are cool enough to handle, peel the peppers and use immediately or freeze for later use.

Guacamole

2	ripe avocados
1	tablespoon lime juice
1	garlic clove, minced
1	tablespoon minced yellow onion
½	ripe tomato, finely chopped
1	jalapeño chile, seeds removed and finely chopped
¼	cup cilantro, finely chopped
	Salt to taste
	Tortilla chips

Place lime juice and chopped garlic in bowl. Cut avocado in half and take out seed. Scoop out avocado and put in bowl with lime juice and smash with fork. Add chopped onion, jalapeño, chile, tomato, and cilantro to the avocado. Mix well and salt to taste if desired. Serve with tortilla chips.

Serves: 6; Calories: 60; Protein: 0 g; Carbohydrate: 4 g; Total fat: 5 g;
Saturated fat: 0 g; Cholesterol: 0 mg; Fiber: 2 g; Sodium: 40 mg

Avocados contain heart-healthy monounsaturated fats.

Hot Artichoke Dip

1   **(14 ounce) can artichoke hearts, drained**

1   **cup fresh Parmesan cheese, grated**

¼   **cup reduced-fat mayonnaise**

2   **cloves garlic, finely chopped**

1   **teaspoon grated lemon peel**

1   **teaspoon Worcestershire sauce**

    Dash of cayenne pepper

    Salt and pepper to taste

    Crackers for serving

Preheat oven to 400°. Place artichoke hearts in the center of 2 thick paper towels; gather up the ends and twist firmly to extract all liquid. In food processor, combine artichokes, Parmesan cheese, mayonnaise, garlic, and spices. Process until smooth, scraping down sides of bowl. Spread mixture in an even layer in small ovenproof dish. Bake for 15 minutes or until hot and lightly golden. Serve warm with crackers.

Serves: 6 (serving size: 3 tablespoons); Calories: 118; Protein: 7 g; Carbohydrate: 6 g; Total fat: 7 g; Saturated fat: 3 g; Cholesterol: 10 mg; Fiber: 0 g; Sodium: 535 mg

OSU is Oklahoma's only university with a statewide presence. The OSU system is comprised of five campuses: OSU-Stillwater, OSU-Okmulgee, OSU-Oklahoma City, OSU-Tulsa, and the OSU Center for Health Sciences in Tulsa, which includes the OSU College of Osteopathic Medicine.

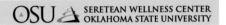
Mediterranean Eggplant Dip

2	medium eggplants
2	tablespoons olive oil
1	medium onion, finely chopped
8	garlic cloves, finely chopped
1	teaspoon turmeric
½	teaspoon salt
¼	teaspoon fresh ground black pepper
3	large tomatoes, peeled and chopped
2	tablespoons tomato paste
3	ounces feta cheese, crumbled
	Garnish with parsley, chopped
	Pita bread

For eggplants, first prick them with fork to prevent bursting. Place eggplant on double thickness of paper towels and cook uncovered at 100% for 12 minutes. Or bake them on sheet pan in preheated 400° oven for 40 minutes or until brown on the outside and soft on the inside (test with a fork). Cool and peel. Mash the pulp.

Sauté onion and garlic in olive oil until brown; stir in turmeric. Add eggplant pulp and sauté for several minutes, stirring frequently. Add salt and pepper. Drop tomatoes into hot water for 1 minute to loosen the skin; cool and then peel. Chop tomatoes into small pieces, and stir them into eggplant mixture with tomato paste. Cook over low heat for 5 minutes, until most of the liquid has evaporated. Transfer to serving platter; garnish with parsley and sprinkle feta cheese on top. This dish can be served hot or cold. Serve with whole-wheat toasted pita bread.

Serves: 6; Calories: 150; Protein: 5 g; Carbohydrate: 17 g; Total fat: 8 g;
Saturated fat: 3 g; Cholesterol: 15 mg; Fiber: 5 g; Sodium: 410 mg

Parmesan Crisps with Caponata and Fresh Basil

Olive oil or pan spray
1   cup fresh Parmesan cheese, grated

Heat non-stick pan on medium high and either brush with little olive oil or lightly apply pan spray. Place 1 tablespoon of Parmesan in pan and flatten into 2-inch circle. Cook for several minutes until cheese stays together enough to be turned over with spatula. Cook for about 1 more minute on other side.

Remove from pan and either cool while flat or shape into cup in small muffin tin while still warm. Yield: 16 crisps

Caponata:
1   tablespoon olive oil
1½   cups eggplant, diced (1 small eggplant)
½   cup red onions, diced
½   cup red bell pepper, diced
1   cup Roma tomatoes, diced
1   tablespoon tomato paste
1   tablespoon minced garlic
2   tablespoons small capers, drained
2   tablespoons red wine vinegar
1½   teaspoons sugar
¼   teaspoon crushed red pepper
¼   cup parsley, minced
Salt and pepper to taste
¼   cup fresh basil, thinly sliced for garnish

Heat large sauté pan over medium and add olive oil. Add eggplant and cook several minutes until partially soft. Add onions, red bell pepper, tomatoes, tomato paste, and garlic and cook for 10 to 15 minutes, stirring occasionally. Remove from heat and add remaining ingredients, (except basil) stirring to combine.

Top each crisp with 2 to 3 tablespoons of caponata and sprinkle with fresh basil.

Serves: 8 (2 crisps per person); Calories: 80; Protein: 5 g; Carbohydrate: 6 g;
Total fat: 5 g; Saturated fat: 2 g; Cholesterol: 10 mg; Fiber: 1 g; Sodium: 270 mg

Pita Toasts

5	pita breads (1 package)
¼	cup olive oil
1	large garlic clove, finely minced
	Salt to taste

Preheat oven to 350°. Cut pita breads crosswise (through the folded edge), forming 2 circles of bread from each pita. Combine olive oil and garlic in small bowl; brush rough side of the bread lightly with oil and garlic mixture. Sprinkle with salt. Stack pitas and cut into triangles (8 triangles per circle).

Spread pita triangles in single layer on 2 sheet pans. Bake pitas until crisp and light brown, about 20 minutes. Rotate baking sheets to make sure pita triangles bake evenly. Serve warm or at room temperature.

Serves: 10; Serving size: 8 pita toasts; Calories: 130; Protein: 3 g; Carbohydrate: 17 g; Total fat: 5 g; Saturated fat: 0 g; Cholesterol: 0 mg; Fiber: 1 g; Sodium: 190 mg

Tomatillo Fruit Salsa with Grilled Shrimp

1	pound tomatillo, husks removed, finely diced
½	cup jicama, finely diced
½	cup mango, finely diced
½	cup red bell pepper, finely diced
¼	cup yellow pepper, finely diced
2	serrano peppers, seeded and finely chopped
¼	cup peanut oil
1	tablespoon extra virgin olive oil
2	tablespoons white wine vinegar
1	tablespoon balsamic vinegar
2	tablespoons lime juice
2	teaspoons lemon juice
¼	cup cilantro, chopped
2	cloves garlic, minced
¼	teaspoon Kosher salt
1	pound large shrimp
¼	teaspoon garlic powder
¼	teaspoon Kosher salt
	Dash of cayenne pepper

Combine the tomatillo, jicama, mango, and peppers in a medium bowl. In another bowl, combine peanut and olive oils, vinegar, lime, and lemon juice. Stir in cilantro, garlic, and salt. Pour over tomatillo mixture and stir to blend. Serve over shrimp.

For the shrimp:

Prepare a gas or charcoal grill. Peel and devein one pound large shrimp. Sprinkle shrimp with garlic powder, coarse salt, and cayenne pepper. Drizzle with olive oil. Grill shrimp until tails curl and turn pink, about 5 to 7 minutes. Serve with fruit salsa.

Serves: 8; Calories: 170; Protein: 12 g; Carbohydrate: 9 g; Total fat: 10 g; Saturated fat: 1.5 g; Cholesterol: 85 mg; Fiber: 2 g; Sodium: 140 mg

Vegetable Quesadillas

Choose 1 or more of the following vegetables:

2	teaspoons olive oil
1	cup finely chopped yellow or red bell peppers
½	cup onion, chopped
8	ounce package fresh mushrooms, chopped
1	zucchini, halved and chopped
1	tomato, diced
	Vegetable oil or cooking spray
½	teaspoon ground cumin
¼	teaspoon salt
¼	teaspoon freshly ground pepper
8	flour tortillas (preferably whole wheat)
6	ounces (1½ cups) reduced-fat Monterey Jack or Cheddar cheese, shredded
	Salsa, low-fat sour cream and guacamole (optional) for garnish
	Serve with Green Salsa, page 131

Heat large skillet over medium. Add olive oil to the hot skillet. Add vegetables and sauté until softened, about 10 minutes. Add cumin, salt, and pepper and stir briefly; transfer mixture to bowl and set aside.

Place a large skillet (preferably nonstick) over medium-high heat until pan is hot. Add a small amount of vegetable oil to the pan or use cooking spray. Add 1 tortilla, and top with ¼ vegetable mixture. Sprinkle with ¼ cup cheese; top with 1 tortilla. Cook 2 minutes on each side or until golden, pressing down with a spatula. Repeat with remaining tortillas, bell pepper mixture, and cheese. Cut tortillas into quarters and serve 2 for appetizer or 4 for dinner. If desired, serve with salsa, low-fat sour cream, and guacamole.

Yield: 8 servings; Calories: 240; Protein: 10 g; Carbohydrate: 32 g; Total fat: 9 g; Saturated fat: 4 g; Cholesterol: 15 mg; Fiber: 3 g; Sodium: 490 mg

---

The OSU Scholar Development Program offers students opportunities to compete for prestigious scholarships and to study abroad. In recent years, students from this program have won Truman, Rhodes, Marshall, Gates, Goldwater, Udall, and Pickering scholarships.

Butternut Squash with Apple Cream

Cranberry Nut Bread

1½	cups whole wheat pastry flour
1½	cups all-purpose white flour
1½	cups granulated sugar
1	tablespoon baking powder
1	teaspoon baking soda
½	teaspoon salt
2	cups fresh cranberries, chopped
1	cup pecans
2	tablespoons grated orange peel
3	large eggs
1½	cups skim milk
⅓	cup canola oil
1	teaspoon pure vanilla

Preheat oven to 350°. Set aside two 8½ x 4½-inch loaf pans; spray with vegetable oil. In a large bowl, mix flour, baking powder, baking soda, and salt. In a separate bowl, mix eggs, milk, oil, orange peel, and sugar. Pour the liquid mixture into the dry ingredients and stir just until moistened. Stir in the cranberries and nuts.

Bake loaves for about 45 minutes or until done. Cool for 10 minutes; remove from pan and let loaves finish cooling before slicing.

Yield: 12 slices per loaf; Calories: 180; Protein: 4 g; Carbohydrate: 27 g; Total fat: 7 g; Saturated fat: .5 g; Cholesterol: 25 mg; Fiber: 2 g; Sodium: 180 mg

Green Chile Cornsticks

¾   **cup all-purpose flour**

¾   **cup yellow cornmeal**

¼   **cup sugar**

2   **teaspoons baking powder**

½   **teaspoon salt**

⅔   **cup low-fat milk**

2   **tablespoons vegetable oil**

1   **large egg, lightly beaten**

8   **ounces frozen corn, thawed**

1   **(4 ounce) can chopped green chiles, drained**

Preheat oven to 400°. Coat cast-iron cornstick pans heavily with cooking spray; place in oven for 10 minutes. Lightly spoon flour into dry measuring cups; level with a knife. Combine flour, cornmeal, sugar, baking powder, and salt; make a well in the center. Combine milk, oil, and egg; add to flour mixture, stirring just until moist. Fold in corn and green chiles.

Spoon batter evenly into preheated pans. Bake at 400° for 20 minutes or until lightly browned. Remove cornsticks from pans immediately; serve warm.

Yield: 14-16; Calories: 100; Protein: 2 g; Carbohydrate: 16 g; Total fat: 3 g;
Saturated fat: .5 g; Cholesterol: 15 mg; Fiber: 1 g; Sodium: 150 mg

This batter can also be made into muffins.

Pagnotta
(Round Country Bread from Central Italy)

Biga "starter":

½ teaspoon Instant Yeast

1¾ cups cool water

3½ cups unbleached bread flour

Measure the flour into a large bowl or mixer if you have a dough hook. Add the yeast and the water and mix until thoroughly combined. Cover tightly and allow it to ferment slowly in the refrigerator for 24 hours before using. To use, scoop out the amount needed and bring to room temperature. The remaining Biga may be saved for about a week or frozen for later use.

Bread:

1 teaspoon Instant Yeast

4 cups unbleached bread flour

3 cups unbleached all-purpose flour

1 tablespoon sea salt

¾ cup Biga

3¼ cups cool water (67-70 degrees)

Additional flour for work surface

Dry polenta or parchment paper for baking surface to prevent sticking

Spray bottle for misting the oven with water

Measure the flour into a large bowl or mixing bowl if you have a dough hook. Add the instant yeast and salt and stir to combine. Add the Biga and slowly add the water with the mixer on low. Continue mixing until the dough becomes smooth and begins to cling to the dough hook and pull away from the sides of the bowl. This is a sticky dough. It will not form a ball and completely pull away from the sides of the bowl. When the dough is completely smooth, remove from the bowl and place on a floured surface. Knead the dough until it is still slightly sticky, but does not stick to the surface when there is a light dusting of flour on it.

(continued)

Pagnotta *(continued)*

Place the dough in a large plastic proofing container with a lid, or a large bowl and cover with plastic. Set the dough rise at room temperature until doubled, 1 ½ to 2 hours, depending on the temperature of the room. Let it rise twice. After the first rising, punch it down by folding the edges into the center and turning it over so the top is once again smooth. Re-cover and let the dough rise a second time until doubled, about an hour. It always rises higher in less time on the second rise.

Turn the dough onto a lightly floured surface. Divide the dough into two equal portions. There will be bubbles in the dough and in the finished loaf. Working with one portion at a time and trying not to over handle the dough, fold the edges in toward the center. Work in a circular motion, folding the entire rim of the dough in toward the center several times to form a round ball with a smooth top and sides.

Sprinkle polenta or put parchment paper on a cookie sheet and place the ball of dough, rough side down, on the sheet. It works best to put each loaf on a separate sheet. Cover and let rise for 40 to 55 minutes. After about 20 minutes, preheat the oven to 425°. If you have a baking stone, place it in the oven before preheating. After about 40 minutes of rising, test the dough by gently pressing your finger into it and removing your finger. If the dough springs back gently, it is ready to bake. If the indention does not spring back, the dough has risen too much and will not "jump" rise in the oven. If this happens, reform the loaves and let rise again for a little less time. When the dough is ready, make an X on the top of each loaf with a serrated knife or razor blade. Mist the tops of the loaves with water from a spray bottle. If you are using a baking stone, slide the loaves onto the stone. If not, place the cookie sheets in the oven and mist again. Bake 5 minutes and mist again. Reduce the temperature to 400°. Bake the loaves until they have a hollow ring when you thump them on the bottom and are a beautiful golden brown on to, 40-50 minutes. They should be dark brown on bottom, especially if you have a baking stone. Remove to a wire rack to cool completely. The bread continues to bake after it is removed from the oven and it will be a sticky, soggy mess in the center if you cut it too soon. It can take up to an hour to cool completely. To preserve the crust overnight place it in a paper bag, don't wrap it with plastic wrap.

Yield: 12 slices per loaf; Calories: 140; Protein: 5 g; Carbohydrate: 30 g; Total fat: 0 g; Saturated fat: 0 g; Cholesterol: 0 mg; Fiber: 1 g; Sodium: 240 mg

---

> *Bread will go stale more rapidly if placed in the refrigerator. For best results, freeze bread or a partial loaf, or keep at room temperature.*

Multi-Grain Rolls

½	cup bulghur wheat
1	cup milk
1	package active dry yeast, or 2 teaspoons instant yeast
⅓	cup honey
2	large eggs, lightly beaten
½	cup quick-cooking oatmeal
1½	cups whole wheat flour
1	teaspoon freshly ground black pepper
1	tablespoon salt
2½-3½	cups all-purpose flour
	Olive oil for brushing tops of rolls
3	tablespoons mixed seeds, such as poppy, sesame, fennel, and÷or oatmeal

Place the bulghur in a medium saucepan with 2 cups water and bring to a boil. Reduce to simmer and cook until the bulghur is tender and the water is absorbed, 12 to 15 minutes.

In the detached bowl of an electric mixer, whisk the warm milk (105°) honey and yeast. If using active dry yeast, set the mixture aside to proof. If using instant yeast you may continue without proofing. Attach the bowl to the mixer fitted with a dough hook and add the bulghur wheat, eggs, oatmeal, whole-wheat flour, pepper, and salt and mix on low speed until combined. Slowly add the all-purpose flour until you form a soft, slightly sticky dough. On medium-low speed, knead dough with dough hook until it springs back when pressed with your finger, about 3 minutes. The dough may also be mixed by hand with a wooden spoon until it reaches this stage. Turn onto a lightly flour dusted surface and knead a few minutes until smooth. Place in an oiled bowl and cover with plastic wrap or in a large plastic proofing container with a lid. Set aside to rise until doubled in size, 1½ to 2 hours depending on the temperature of the room.

Generously oil two 8-inch round cake pans. Measure the dough into 2 ounce portions and form each portion into a ball, placing 11 in each pan. Brush the tops generously with olive oil. Cover with plastic wrap and set aside to rise until half again as large, 20-25 minutes. Preheat oven to 375°. Sprinkle the tops of the rolls with your choice of seeds. Bake until dark golden brown on top, 20 to 22 minutes. Cool slightly before unmolding. Serve immediately.

Serves: 22; Calories: 145; Protein: 4.5 g; Carbohydrates: 28 g; Total fat: 1.5 g;
Saturated fat: 0 g; Cholesterol: 20 mg; Fiber: 2.5 g; Sodium: 265 mg

Beet Soup

2	tablespoons light olive oil
2	celery stalks, sliced thin on the bias
1	medium onion, sliced thin
3	garlic cloves, sliced
1	small rutabaga, (peeled), julienne
1	large carrot, julienne
1	medium red potato, julienne
3	medium beets, peeled, julienne
8	cups vegetable stock
1	teaspoon kosher salt
	Pinch ground black pepper
1	teaspoon dried dill weed
	Light sour cream for garnish

In large stockpot, heat olive oil. Add all vegetables and sauté about 10 minutes or until vegetables are softened. Add vegetable stock, salt, pepper, and dill. Simmer the soup over low heat until all vegetables are tender. Serve with a dollop light sour cream on top.

Serves: 8; Calories: 100; Protein: 2 g; Carbohydrates: 15 g; Total fat: 3.5 g; Saturated fat: 0 mg; Cholesterol: 0 mg; Fiber: 4 g; Sodium: 310 mg

OSU's Math Department has been recognized by the American Mathematics Association as one of four innovative programs in the nation. The department has produced five Sloan Fellows, comparable to the status of MIT.

Black Bean Chili

2   tablespoons olive oil

1   large onion, diced

2   celery stalks, diced

1   poblano or jalapeño chile, minced

4   large garlic cloves, minced

1   tablespoon cumin, ground

1   tablespoon dried oregano leaves

1   teaspoon ground red chilies (New Mexico) or 2 teaspoons chili powder and ¼ teaspoon cayenne pepper

1   (15-ounce) can tomatoes (no salt), puréed in blender

1   (15-ounce) can low-sodium chicken or vegetable broth or 2 cups homemade stock

2   (15-ounce) cans black beans, rinsed and drained

    Cooked rice

    Fresh cilantro or Cilantro Pesto, page 131

    Light sour cream

Heat the oil in a large skillet and sauté the onions, celery, and pepper over medium heat until they soften. Add the garlic, cumin, oregano and ground chilies or chili powder and cook another 5 minutes. Add the puréed tomatoes, chicken stock and black beans and simmer chili partially covered for 25 minutes. Using a kitchen blender, purée 1 cup chili until smooth. Stir it back into the pot of chili. Simmer an additional 10 minutes. Serve 1 cup chili on ⅓ cup rice. Sprinkle with fresh, chopped cilantro or Cilantro Pesto and sour cream.

Serves: 4; Calories: 250; Protein: 12 g; Carbohydrate: 34 g; Total fat: 9 g;
Saturated fat: 1.5 g; Cholesterol: 0 mg; Fiber: 11 g; Sodium: 100 mg

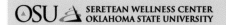

Butternut Squash with Apple Cream

3	tablespoons canola or olive oil
4	leeks (white and pale green parts only) washed and chopped
1	large carrot, diced
2½	pounds butternut squash, peeled, seeded, cut into bite-size pieces (6-7 cups)
2	sweet apples, peeled, cored, chopped
1½	teaspoons dried thyme
½	teaspoon dried sage
	Salt and pepper to taste
3½	cups chicken broth, vegetable broth, or water
½	cup milk (optional)
1½	cups apple cider or natural apple juice, divided
½	cup light sour cream
	Garnish: chopped fresh chives

Heat oil in large saucepan over medium-high heat. Add leeks and carrots; sauté until slightly softened, about 15 minutes. Mix in squash, apples, thyme, and sage. Stir vegetables together; add stock and 1 cup apple juice and bring to a simmer. Cover and cook until vegetables are tender, stirring occasionally, about 30 minutes. Cool slightly.

Working in small batches, purée half of the soup in a blender adding the milk or an additional ½ cup water if needed to thin soup. Return soup to the pan and mix together. In a small saucepan, heat remaining ½ cup apple juice until reduced to ¼ cup, about 5 to 10 minutes. Cool. Place sour cream in small bowl and whisk in the reduced juice or cider. Ladle soup into bowls. Drizzle with apple cream and sprinkle with chopped chives.

Yield: 9-10 cups; Serves: 6; Calories: 270; Protein: 5 g; Carbohydrate: 45 g;
Total fat: 9 g; Saturated fat: 2.5 g; Cholesterol: 10 mg; Fiber: 8 g; Sodium: 250 mg

---

Chicken Noodle Soup

1	pound skinless, boneless, chicken breasts
2	tablespoons olive oil
1	medium onion, finely chopped
2	medium-size carrots, peeled and finely chopped
4	stalks celery, finely chopped
½	teaspoon salt
1	teaspoon pepper
8	cups good quality chicken broth, low-sodium
2	cups frozen egg noodles
	Parsley, chopped for garnish

Cover the chicken with water in a medium saucepan and cook on low until tender, about 15 minutes. Remove from pan and when cool enough to handle, cut or shred into pieces. Reserve the cooking liquid and use it as part of the chicken broth.

Heat stockpot over medium-low heat; add olive oil. When oil is hot, add onions, celery and carrots, salt and pepper; cook until tender (about 15 minutes).

Add the stock to the pot and heat until simmering. Add chicken and pasta and simmer gently for about 25 minutes. Garnish with chopped parsley.

Serves: 8; Calories: 250; Protein: 24 g; Carbohydrates: 19 g; Total fat: 8 g;
Saturated fat: 2 g; Cholesterol: 75 mg; Fiber: 3 g; Sodium: 350 mg

*Princeton Review named OSU as one of the best
higher educational institutions in the western United States.*

Classic Gazpacho

2	large tomatoes (about 1 pound)
1	large cucumber, peeled, halved lengthwise, seeded
1	medium red onion
1	red bell pepper, roasted and peeled
3	cups tomato juice
½	cup chopped fresh cilantro
⅓	cup red wine vinegar
2	tablespoons olive oil
⅛	teaspoon hot pepper sauce

Cut tomato, cucumber, and onion into 1-inch pieces and transfer to food processor or blender. Add bell pepper and purée. Transfer to bowl. Add tomato juice, cilantro, vinegar, oil and hot pepper sauce. Season with salt and pepper to taste. Refrigerate until cold. Soup can be prepared 2 days ahead. Serve the soup cold in chilled glasses or bowls; place the cucumber relish on top.

Cucumber Relish:

1	large cucumber
½	red onion, peeled
1	green bell pepper
2	tablespoons rice wine vinegar
2	tablespoons olive oil
	Salt and pepper to taste

Wash all the vegetables. Cut the cucumber lengthwise and seed. Cut into strips and dice. Dice the red onion and chop the green onion. Cut the bell pepper into strips and dice. To make vinaigrette, mix olive oil and vinegar together; blend well. Season to taste with salt and pepper. Add the vinaigrette to the relish.

Serves: 6; Calories: 160; Protein: 2 g; Carbohydrate: 16 g; Total fat: 10 g;
Saturated fat: 1.5 g; Cholesterol: 0 mg; Fiber: 3 g; Sodium: 230 mg

Corn Bisque

1	tablespoon canola oil
1	tablespoon butter
2	cups onion, chopped
2	whole carrots, diced
2	stalks celery, diced
1	red bell pepper, diced
5	cups fresh or frozen corn, (thawed) divided (reserve 1 cup)
2	teaspoons fresh rosemary
⅛	teaspoon cayenne pepper
4	cups low-sodium chicken stock
⅓	cup half-and-half or low-fat milk

Heat butter and oil in heavy large pot over medium heat. Add carrots, onions, red bell pepper and celery. Sauté for 10 minutes or until vegetables are soft. Add 4 cups corn, rosemary, and cayenne pepper and sauté for 2 minutes. Pour stock in with the vegetables. Reduce heat to low and simmer uncovered about 30 minutes.

Working in batches, purée soup in the blender. Return soup to the pot and mix in half-and-half and 1 cup of corn. Season to taste with salt and pepper.

Serves: 8; Calories: 175; Protein: 7 g; Carbohydrate: 26 g; Total fat: 6 g;
Saturated fat: 2.5 g; Cholesterol: 11 mg; Fiber: 4 g; Sodium: 140 mg

To use fresh corn, husk about 5 ears of corn and wash well. Cut the kernels off the husk with a sharp knife, and reserve 1 cup. Add the uncooked corn to the soup and simmer with the rest of the vegetables. After puréeing the soup, add the 1 cup of reserved corn and simmer soup an additional 5 to 10 minutes. This method is excellent when fresh corn is available at your local farmer's market.

Cream of Tomato Soup

1	large onion, chopped (about 1 cup)
2	garlic cloves, minced
1	tablespoon olive oil
1	red pepper, diced
2	pounds tomatoes, 2 (15-ounce) cans, unsalted or fresh tomatoes, skin removed
½	cup dry white wine
2	cups low-sodium chicken stock
⅛	teaspoon ground chiles or cayenne pepper
1	teaspoon oregano
⅓	cup half-and-half or low-fat milk
	Salt and pepper to taste

Heat olive oil in large pan; sauté onions and garlic until tender, about 15 minutes. Add tomatoes, roasted red pepper, chicken stock, white wine, chiles, pinch of salt, and oregano and simmer for about 30 to 45 minutes. Working in batches, purée soup in blender adding the milk or half and half. Return to pot and stir until heated through. Season to taste with salt and pepper. Garnish each bowl with chopped parsley and croutons if desired.

Serves: 6; Calories: 120; Protein: 4 g; Carbohydrate: 14 g; Total fat: 5 g;
Saturated fat: 1.5 g; Cholesterol: 6 mg; Fiber: 3 g; Sodium: 175 mg

*To peel tomatoes for cooking, drop them in boiling water for 10 to 15 seconds.
Remove the tomatoes with a slotted spoon and let rest until cool enough to handle.
The skin should easily slip off.*

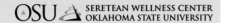

Curried Vegetable Soup

1   tablespoon olive oil

2   Yukon gold potatoes (½ pound), diced

4   garlic cloves, chopped

1   tablespoon mild Indian curry paste (Patak)

1   sweet onion, diced

4   cups low sodium vegetable stock

1   zucchini, cut into thin strips (remove seeds, mostly want color from skin)

1   yellow squash, cut into thin strips (remove seeds, mostly want color from skin)

½   teaspoon salt (or more to taste)

In a stockpot, heat olive oil. Add the onions and sauté until golden brown. Add garlic, sauté until light brown; add potatoes and curry, sauté until curry is well incorporated. Add vegetable stock and cook until potatoes are soft. Remove from heat, let cool a little, and purée. Return soup to heat; add zucchini and yellow squash. Cook until soft. Salt to taste and serve.

Serves: 6; Calories: 140; Protein: 4 g; Carbohydrate: 26 g; Total fat: 3 g;
Saturated fat: 0 g; Cholesterol: 0 mg; Fiber: 3 g; Sodium: 480 mg

Hot and Sour Soup

4	ounces chicken breast
1½	teaspoons salt, divided
2	tablespoons cornstarch, divided
8	cups low-sodium chicken stock, preferably homemade
3	dried black or shiitake mushrooms
2	tablespoons wood ear mushrooms
¾	cup bamboo shoots
1	carrot, sliced into match sticks
12	ounces soft tofu
1	green onion
1	slice gingerroot, peeled and minced
2	teaspoons soy sauce
2	teaspoons vinegar
2	eggs
1	teaspoon sesame oil
	Hot sauce to taste
	Black pepper to taste
	Chopped cilantro as a garnish

Soak the wood ear mushrooms and black mushrooms in warm water for 30 minutes. Drain and rinse; cut into slivers. Cut chicken into thin shreds the size of matches. Mix with ½ teaspoon salt and 2 teaspoons cornstarch. Cut all vegetables and tofu into uniform pieces (same as chicken). Bring stock to a boil. Add chicken to soup followed by sliced mushrooms and vegetables. Cook for 3 minutes; add soy sauce, vinegar, salt, and remaining cornstarch mixed with 2 tablespoons cold water. Simmer until soup is slightly thickened.

Beat eggs and pour into bubbling soup very slowly stirring in one direction. If possible, use funnel with a small opening so the eggs fall through in a thin thread. Add sesame oil, hot sauce, pepper, chopped cilantro, and serve immediately.

Serves: 8; Calories: 120; Protein: 11 g; Carbohydrate: 8 g; Total fat: 5 g;
Saturated fat: 1.5 g; Cholesterol: 65 mg; Fiber: 1 g; Sodium: 620 mg

Potato Leek Soup

2	tablespoons vegetable oil
1	small onion, diced
3	small or 2 large leeks, white and pale green part only, rinsed well, diced
3	cups low-sodium chicken or vegetable stock
1	cup water
2	pounds white potatoes, peeled and diced
3	tablespoons half-and-half
¼	cup parsley, chopped plus extra for garnish
	Salt and pepper to taste

Heat the oil in a large saucepan; sauté onion, and leeks until softened, about 10 minutes. Add chicken broth, water, and potatoes to the sautéed vegetables. Bring the soup to simmer and continue to cook about 20 minutes or until the potatoes are tender.

Blend half the soup (in batches) in a kitchen blender with the parsley and half and half until creamy. Pour the blended soup back into the saucepan with the rest of the soup. Season to taste with salt and pepper. Garnish with chopped fresh parsley.

Serves: 6; Calories: 240; Protein: 6 g; Carbohydrate: 42 g; Total fat: 7 g;
Saturated fat: 1.5 g; Cholesterol: 5 mg; Fiber: 3 g; Sodium: 270 mg

Red Lentil Soup

1   tablespoon olive oil

1   large leek (white part only), or small onion, chopped

3   large garlic cloves, minced

2   stalks celery, chopped

2   carrots, chopped

1   (15-ounce) can low-sodium tomatoes, purée in blender with juices

1   zucchini, diced

¾   cup lentils red (brown can be substituted)

4   cups vegetable or chicken stock

2   cups water

       Salt and pepper to taste

In a large pot, heat oil over medium heat. Add leek or onion, celery, carrots and garlic. Stir frequently until the vegetables are soft, 8 to 10 minutes. Add tomatoes, stock, water, zucchini and lentils. Season soup with salt and pepper. Bring soup to a simmer and cook, partially covered, until lentils are tender, about 20 minutes (45 minutes if using brown lentils).

Serves: 8; Calories: 110; Protein: 6 g; Carbohydrate: 18 g; Total fat: 2 g;
Saturated fat: 0 g; Cholesterol: 0 mg; Fiber: 7 g; Sodium: 30 mg

Roasted Tomato Soup

2	tablespoons olive oil, divided
	Salt and pepper to taste
8	cloves garlic, skins on
1	medium yellow onion, diced
1	teaspoon dried basil
½	teaspoon oregano
6	cups chicken stock
18	Roma tomatoes
3	tablespoons half-and-half
	Parmesan cheese, optional garnish
	Salt and pepper to taste

Preheat oven to 400°. Remove stem ends of tomatoes and cut in half lengthwise. Lay tomatoes on parchment-lined baking sheet and drizzle with 1 tablespoon olive oil and season with salt and pepper. Place unwrapped garlic cloves on sheet as well.

Roast garlic for about 20 minutes until soft, and remove from pan; continue roasting tomatoes for another 25 minutes. Remove skin on garlic.

Sauté onion in soup pot with 1 tablespoon olive oil for about 10 minutes. Add tomatoes, roasted garlic, and herbs to the pot. Add chicken stock and simmer about 20 minutes.

Purée soup in blender, adjust consistency to your liking with extra stock or water. Add cream. Season with salt and pepper. Garnish with Parmesan cheese.

Serves: 6; Calories: 130; Protein: 5 g; Carbohydrate: 14 g; Total fat: 7 g;
Saturated fat: 2 g; Cholesterol: 10 mg; Fiber: 3 g; Sodium: 130 mg

Spring Asparagus Soup

1	pound fresh asparagus
1	tablespoon butter
1	tablespoon olive oil
3	leeks, white parts only, washed and thinly sliced
1	small (¼ pound) potato
½	teaspoon salt
4	cups low-sodium vegetable or chicken stock
3	tablespoons half-and-half
	Salt and pepper to taste
	Parmesan cheese, grated for garnish

Cut off the tips of the asparagus and set aside. Break off the bottoms of asparagus (about 1-inch) and save for stock or discard. Roughly chop the stems of the remaining asparagus. Melt butter in soup pot; add oil. Stir in the leeks, and cook them over medium-high heat for several minutes. Add the potatoes, asparagus stems, salt, and stock. Bring to a boil; then cook at a simmer until the asparagus and potatoes are just tender, about 6 to 10 minutes. Blend the soup well adding the cream. Return it to the stove and season with salt and pepper if needed. Cook the asparagus tips separately in boiling water for 1 to 2 minutes and drain. Garnish the soup with asparagus tips and grated Parmesan cheese.

Serves: 6; Calories: 140; Protein: 6 g; Carbohydrate: 14 g; Total fat: 7 g; Saturated fat: 3 g; Cholesterol: 15 mg; Fiber: 3 g; Sodium: 340 mg

---

There is only one active coach (Bob Knight) ranked ahead of OSU Men's Basketball Coach Eddie Sutton in both victories and winning percentage, and OSU's boss ranks behind only Dean Smith in victories through 33 or fewer years of coaching.

Sweet Potato and Chipotle Soup

2   pounds sweet potatoes, peeled and cut into large dice

1   medium onion, diced

2   teaspoons olive oil

2   garlic cloves, sliced

6   cups chicken or vegetable stock (homemade or canned low-sodium)

½   chipotle pepper (smoked jalapeño), canned

1   teaspoon brown sugar

1   tablespoon fresh lime juice

1   teaspoon salt

     Black pepper to taste

     Cilantro (chopped) and light sour cream for garnish

Heat large saucepan with oil on medium heat and add onion. Sauté several minutes or until light brown. Add the garlic and stir briefly; add the sweet potatoes, chipotle, chicken or vegetable stock, and only half teaspoon of salt.

Bring to a boil, then turn down heat and simmer until potatoes are tender, about 30 minutes. Remove from heat and let cool a bit. Purée in batches with either hand-held blender or standard blender. Add enough stock or water until desired consistency. Return soup to the pan and reheat if necessary. Add brown sugar, lime juice, remaining half teaspoon salt, and the pepper to taste. Garnish with cilantro and a swirl of sour cream.

Serves: 8; Calories: 140; Protein: 4 g; Carbohydrate: 27 g; Total fat: 2.5 g;
Saturated fat: 1 g; Cholesterol: 5 mg; Fiber: 2 g; Sodium: 380 mg

Vegetable Soup with Fresh Basil

1	tablespoon olive oil
2	carrots, peeled and diced
3	garlic cloves, minced
2	stalks celery, diced
1	small onion, diced
1	(15-ounce) can low-sodium tomatoes, puréed in blender or food processor with juice
4	cups low-sodium chicken broth
1	cup water
1	potato, peeled and diced
1	cup butternut squash, peeled and cut into small dice
2	zucchini, diced
	Handful of fresh basil
	Parmesan cheese, optional for garnish

Heat olive oil in heavy pot over medium heat. Add carrots, garlic, celery and onion. Sauté about 10 minutes. Add tomatoes, chicken stock, water, potato and butternut squash. Partially cover and simmer for 30 minutes. Add the zucchini to the soup and continue to simmer for an additional 10 minutes. Blend 1 cup of soup with fresh basil leaves. Add the blended soup back to the pot and stir. Serve with Parmesan cheese.

Serves: 6; Calories: 115; Protein: 4 g; Carbohydrate: 19 g; Total fat 2.5 g;
Saturated fat: 0 g; Cholesterol: 0 mg; Fiber: 4 g; Sodium: 215 mg

White Bean and Chicken Chowder

1	tablespoon olive oil
½	cup onion, diced
3	cloves garlic, minced
½	cup celery, diced
½	cup carrots, diced
1	teaspoon ground cumin
½	teaspoon dried thyme
1	tablespoon flour
4	cups low-sodium chicken stock
½	cup corn
1	(15-ounce) can cannellini or white beans
½	pound chicken breasts, cooked and shredded
1	(4-ounce) can diced green chiles
	Salt and black pepper to taste
	Cilantro for garnish

Heat a 2-quart pan; add olive oil, and then onion, garlic, celery, and carrots; sauté vegetables for ten minutes over medium heat. Add the cumin and thyme and sauté several minutes. Stir flour into sautéed vegetables. Slowly whisk in chicken stock. Add the corn, beans, chili peppers, and season with salt if desired. Simmer for about 30 minutes. Add cooked chicken and simmer chowder until heated through. Serve with chopped cilantro.

Serves: 8; Calories: 180; Protein: 23 g; Carbohydrate: 14 g; Total fat: 4 g; Saturated fat: 0 g; Cholesterol: 50 mg; Fiber: 4 g; Sodium: 350 mg

Curried Chicken Salad

1½	pounds boneless, skinless chicken breasts
½	cup light mayonnaise
⅓	cup nonfat plain yogurt
5	teaspoons curry powder
1½	tablespoons fresh lime juice
1	teaspoon honey
½	teaspoon ground ginger
¼	teaspoon salt
¼	teaspoon fresh ground black pepper
½	small red onion, diced
1	cup seedless red grapes, halved
½	cup unsalted cashews, coarsely chopped

Bake or poach chicken breasts until done, about 15 minutes. When cool enough to handle, cut into bite-size pieces. To make dressing, combine the mayonnaise, yogurt, curry powder, lime juice, honey, ginger, salt, and pepper.

In a large bowl, combine chicken, onion, grapes, and dressing. Serve chicken salad on a bed of lettuce greens with cashews sprinkled on top.

Serves: 6; Calories: 290; Protein: 29 g; Carbohydrate: 13 g; Total fat: 13 g;
Saturated fat: 2.5 g; Cholesterol: 75 mg; Fiber: 1 g; Sodium: 340 mg

---

*Oklahoma State won the first NCAA wrestling championship and
has won 31 such trophies since — more than any other school in the country.
The Cowboys have won 842 dual meets, lost only 87 and tied 20 in 82 years of varsity competition.*

Grilled Turkey Burgers

2	teaspoons olive oil
1	small red onion, diced
2	cloves garlic, minced
1½	pounds extra-lean ground turkey
6	tablespoons bread crumbs
1	egg
¼	cup ketchup
1	tablespoon Worcestershire sauce
1	teaspoon dried herbs (thyme, basil, or oregano)
¼	teaspoon cayenne pepper
¼	teaspoon salt
¼	teaspoon pepper
6	whole wheat buns

Heat a small pan to medium and add a small amount of olive oil. Briefly sauté the onion and garlic for about 2 to 3 minutes. In a large bowl, combine the turkey, onion, garlic, and remaining ingredients and mix well.

Form into 6 patties; chill for about 15 minutes. Meanwhile, heat an outdoor grill or grill pan. Brush each burger with olive oil and grill for about 5 to 6 minutes per side or until cooked through. Serve on whole wheat buns with desired accompaniments.

Serves: 6; Calories: 180; Protein: 30 g; Carbohydrate: 10 g; Total fat: 3 g; Saturated fat: 0 g; Cholesterol: 80 mg; Fiber: 0 g; Sodium: 370 mg

Layered Enchiladas

1	teaspoon vegetable oil
1	pound lean ground turkey breast
½	large onion (1 cup), diced
2	garlic cloves, minced
1	jalapeño chile, diced
2	tablespoons chili powder
	Salt and pepper to taste
1	(15 ounce) can chili beans
6	corn tortillas, each torn into 4 pieces
1½	cups (5 ounces) grated low-fat Cheddar cheese
1	(15-ounce) can Mexican stewed tomatoes, puréed in blender
	Fresh chopped cilantro to taste (optional)

Preheat oven to 300°. Lightly oil a 9 x 9-inch glass baking dish. In a large skillet, heat oil and sauté meat, onion, garlic, and jalapeño until meat is cooked, about 10 minutes. Reduce heat to low. Mix in chili powder and cook for 5 minutes more. Season mixture with salt and pepper.

Spoon half the meat mixture, then half the beans evenly over bottom of prepared dish. Overlap half the tortillas to cover meat and beans completely. Repeat with 1 more layer of meat, beans, and tortillas. Sprinkle cheese over top. Pour puréed tomatoes over the cheese. Bake the casserole until heated through and bubbling at the edges, about 30 minutes. Garnish with cilantro.

Serves 6; Calories: 340; Protein: 38 g; Carbohydrate: 35 g; Total fat: 7 g;
Saturated fat: 3 g; Cholesterol: 80 mg; Fiber: 6 g; Sodium: 820 mg

---

Extra lean ground beef can be substituted for the turkey.

Lemon Chicken

1	pound boneless, skinless chicken breasts
2	tablespoons olive oil
3	tablespoons Dijon mustard
3	tablespoons fresh squeezed lemon juice
1	teaspoon dried tarragon, basil or oregano

Wash the chicken and pat dry with paper towels. Put the chicken between sheets of wax paper and pound with mallet or rolling pin until even thickness. Place chicken in a shallow glass-baking pan.

Preheat oven to 350°. In a small bowl, whisk together the olive oil, mustard, lemon juice, and tarragon. Pour it over the chicken and bake uncovered for 40 to 45 minutes.

Slice the cooked chicken on the diagonal and serve one chicken breast or 4 ounces per person. Serve over pasta, rice or potatoes and spoon some of the sauce over each serving.

Serves: 4; Calories: 175; Protein: 27 g; Carbohydrate: 1 g; Total fat: 6 g;
Saturated fat: 1 g; Cholesterol: 65 mg; Fiber: 1 g; Sodium: 115 mg

*Most of the fat in olive oil is monounsaturated, a fat that may help lower
LDL cholesterol (the bad kind) and lower triglycerides. Olive oil also has a higher amount of
linoleic acid compared to other cooking oils, an essential nutrient which must be obtained through diet.
Olive oil is naturally high in Vitamin E. It is the preferred oil to use for a heart-healthy Mediterranean diet.*

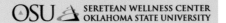
Mediterranean Chicken with Lemons, Olives and Potatoes

2   **pounds boneless, skinless chicken breast (cut each breast into 3-4 pieces)**

½   **cup minced cilantro**

½   **cup minced flat leaf parsley**

2   **tablespoons minced garlic**

1   **tablespoon minced fresh ginger**

1   **tablespoon ground black pepper**

½   **teaspoon salt**

¼   **teaspoon saffron threads**

1   **fresh lemon, quartered (or whole preserved lemon—see recipe—omit salt if using preserved lemon)**

2   **medium onions, sliced thin**

1   **pound red or white potatoes, cut into thin wedges**

1   **tablespoon sweet paprika**

⅓   **cup olive oil**

⅓   **cup water**

1   **cup Kalamata olives, pitted and cut in half**

In a heavy pot or skillet large enough to hold all of the chicken and other ingredients, mix the cilantro, parsley, garlic, ginger, pepper and salt. Crumble the saffron into the herbs. Add one fresh lemon or preserved lemon into the mixture. Mix the seasonings together well. Add the chicken and rub with herbs well until each piece is coated.

Combine the paprika and potatoes. Cover the chicken with sliced onions and potatoes. Pour the olive oil over the top. Add the water. Cover and bake in a 350° oven for 45 minutes or until potatoes are soft. Serve on a platter, garnish with the olives and slices of the preserved lemon if using.

Serves: 8; Calories: 330; Protein: 29 g; Carbohydrate: 18 g; Total fat: 16 g; Saturated fat: 2 g; Cholesterol: 65 mg; Fiber: 3 g; Sodium: 390 mg

(continued)

Mediterranean Chicken with Lemons, Olives and Potatoes *(continued)*

Preserved Lemons:

12   whole lemons

1   cup sea salt

Fill a scrupulously clean gallon jar with boiling water. Leave for 10 minutes or so.

Cut the lemons into quarters but leaving the quarters attached at the bottom end. Open the lemon slightly and pack the lemon with salt. Then press the lemon to the bottom of the jar. Do this with all the lemons. Press them firmly so they will yield up a considerable amount of juice. Fill up the jar to the top with an inch to spare. If there is not enough juice so the lemons are covered completely add the juice of more lemons. Add another tablespoon of salt to the top. Cover and let stand in the refrigerator for at least 3 weeks. Every few days, turn the jar upside down to help distribute the juices evenly. Preserved lemons will last up to 6 months refrigerated.

*Chicken thighs can be substituted for the breast meat; cooking time will be about 30 minutes longer with bone in meat. Remove skin before cooking.

*Olives are an excellent source of heart-healthy monounsaturated fats.

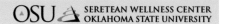

Moroccan Chicken Salad with Green Beans

2   **pounds boneless, skinless chicken breasts**

1   **teaspoon olive oil**

¼   **teaspoon salt**

¼   **teaspoon pepper**

1   **red bell pepper, thinly sliced**

½   **cup red onion, thinly sliced**

1½   **cups green beans, cut into 1-inch pieces**

¼   **cup chopped, fresh Italian parsley**

Dressing (makes about 1 cup):

1   **clove garlic, minced**

1   **teaspoon ground cumin**

3   **tablespoons fresh squeezed lemon juice**

2   **tablespoons red wine vinegar**

⅓   **cup chicken stock**

⅓   **cup olive oil**

½   **cup fresh cilantro leaves**

¼   **teaspoon cayenne, more or less to taste**

    Salt and pepper to taste

Rub chicken breasts with olive oil; season lightly with salt and pepper. Roast the chicken breasts at 375° for about 20 to 25 minutes until done. An instant thermometer should read 165°. Cool the chicken then shred into bite-sized pieces. Cook the sliced green beans in boiling water for about 1 minute. Combine the salad ingredients.

For the dressing, combine the first 6 ingredients with a whisk, blender or food processor. Add the cayenne, salt, and pepper to taste. Pour dressing over salad and combine. You may not need all of the dressing.

Serves: 8; Calories: 240; Protein: 27 g; Carbohydrate: 4 g; Total fat: 12 g;
Saturated fat: 1.5 g; Cholesterol: 65 mg; Fiber: 1 g; Sodium: 180 mg

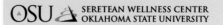

Murghi Tikka
(Chicken Kabobs)

1½   **pounds boneless, skinless chicken breasts (cut into cubes)**

Marinade:

1   **cup plain low-fat yogurt**

2   **tablespoons oil**

3   **garlic cloves, minced**

2   **tablespoons fresh lemon juice**

1   **1-inch piece fresh ginger, minced**

1   **teaspoon ground turmeric**

1   **teaspoon ground coriander**

1   **tablespoon ground cumin**

½   **teaspoon salt**

½   **teaspoon chili powder (or to taste)**

1   **tablespoon paprika**

      Freshly ground pepper

2   **tablespoons fresh cilantro, chopped for garnish**

      Lemon wedges

Mix all ingredients for marinade in a 1-quart glass bowl. Add chicken and coat well. Cover with plastic wrap and leave in refrigerator overnight. Thread chicken pieces on skewers. Grill over hot charcoal or under broiler, turning until golden on all sides. Serve on hot platter and sprinkle with cilantro and lemon wedges.

Serves: 6; Calories: 160; Protein: 22 g; Carbohydrate: 4 g; Total fat: 6 g;
Saturated fat: 1 g; Cholesterol: 50 mg; Fiber: 0 g; Sodium: 470 mg

---

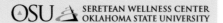
Pan-Seared Chicken Breast with Peach Chutney

2   tablespoons olive oil

6   boneless, skinless chicken breasts, (about 6 ounces each)

        Salt and pepper to taste

3   tablespoons lemon zest

Peach Chutney:

3   tablespoons sugar with 3 tablespoons water

2   peaches, skinned and chopped

½   red onion, chopped

½   cup golden raisins

1   garlic clove, minced (about 1 teaspoon)

¼   cup roasted red pepper, chopped

4   tablespoons rice wine vinegar

For the chutney, place the sugar÷water mixture in a sauce pan and let the sugar cook for 5 minutes. Place the other ingredients in the pan and cook for 15 minutes. Strain the liquid off and reduce just the liquid to thick syrup. Pour the syrup over the chutney mixture and chill.

To prepare the chicken, pour the olive oil in a preheated pan and place the breasts in to sauté. Flip each breast over and season with pepper, salt, and lemon zest. Cook until 165° or about 10 minutes. To serve, place one chicken breast on each plate and top with a spoonful of peach chutney.

Serves: 6; Calories: 310; Protein: 40 g; Carbohydrate: 21 g; Total fat: 7 g;
Saturated fat: 1 g; Cholesterol: 100 mg; Fiber: 1 g; Sodium: 115 mg

Parmesan Chicken

¼   cup Italian bread crumbs (or plain to reduce sodium)
¼   cup Parmesan cheese, grated
     Fresh ground pepper to taste
⅓   cup Italian salad dressing
1   pound boneless, skinless chicken breasts
     Fresh thyme, basil or oregano, minced (optional)

Preheat oven to 350°. Combine Italian bread crumbs, Parmesan cheese, and pepper in a shallow bowl. Pour salad dressing into another bowl. Wash chicken and trim off all fat. Put chicken between plastic wrap and lightly pound with rolling pin or meat mallet until it is an even thickness. Dip each chicken breast in the dressing; roll in the bread crumbs. Season to taste with fresh herbs if desired.

Place chicken in a lightly oiled shallow sheet pan or glass baking dish. Bake uncovered for 40 minutes. Slice chicken breasts into strips and serve.

Serves: 4; Calories: 200; Protein: 26 g; Carbohydrate: 7 g; Total fat: 7 g;
Saturated fat: 2 g; Cholesterol: 60 mg; Fiber: 0 g; Sodium: 525 mg

The real Pistol Pete was Frank Eaton, a U.S. marshal from Perkins, Oklahoma.

Sweet and Spicy Barbecued Chicken

½	cup light brown sugar
¼	cup cider vinegar
2	tablespoons olive oil
2	tablespoons lemon juice
3	garlic cloves
1½	tablespoons Dijon mustard
1	teaspoon Worcestershire sauce
½	teaspoon salt
6	boneless, skinless chicken breasts (1½ pounds)

In a blender, combine the brown sugar, vinegar, olive oil, lemon juice, garlic cloves, mustard, lime juice, and Worcestershire sauce. Blend until smooth. Lightly pound chicken breasts between sheets of plastic wrap. Arrange chicken breasts in a large glass baking dish. Pour the marinade over the chicken and refrigerate for 1 hour or up to 3 hours, turning occasionally.

Prepare a gas or charcoal grill. Remove the chicken from the marinade and grill until browned and cooked through (about 4 to 5 minutes per side). Serve hot or at room temperature.

Serves: 6; Calories: 275; Protein: 33 g; Carbohydrate: 20 g; Total fat: 6 g;
Saturated fat: 1 g; Cholesterol: 80 mg; Fiber: 0 g; Sodium: 130 mg

*Although the recipe was analyzed using all the marinade ingredients,
some of the marinade stays in the pan and is not actually consumed.
As a result, the calories, carbohydrate, fat, and sodium are less than the actual analysis.*

Tofu Hunan Style
with Napa Cabbage and Carrots

1	pound firm tofu (bean curd)
1	carrot, sliced very thin
2	green onions, sliced thin
½	Napa cabbage, sliced in thin strips
2	tablespoons canola or peanut oil, divided
2	tablespoons cornstarch
½	cup cold water
1	tablespoon soy sauce
¼	teaspoon salt
1	tablespoon hot bean sauce
1	tablespoon sesame oil
½	teaspoon black pepper
2-3	hot red peppers, whole (optional)
	Cooked white rice

Cut the tofu into ½-inch squares. Thinly slice the carrot, onion, and cabbage. Heat 1 tablespoon oil and stir-fry vegetables together for 2 minutes. Remove from pan and set aside. Heat 1 tablespoon oil in the skillet and stir-fry tofu for 2 minutes.

Mix cornstarch with cold water and set aside. Add the remaining ingredients to the pan, and stir-fry all together for a few minutes until hot. Pour in the cornstarch mixture and cook for 1 to 2 minutes more. Remove to plate and serve over rice.

Serves: 4; Calories: 200; Protein: 9 g; Carbohydrate: 10 g; Total fat: 13 g;
Saturated fat: 1 g; Cholesterol: 0 mg; Fiber: 1 g Sodium: 890 mg

The Gardiner Art Gallery in the Bartlett Center for Visual Arts first opened in 1965 and has grown to become an integral part of the department's teaching environment as well as a place for the university and general community to experience the visual arts. Exhibits have varied from local, such as annual student and faculty exhibitions, to national shows like the biennial Cimarron National Works on Paper Exhibition, to international offerings of Japanese and German prints, and a sand painting (mandala) created by Tibetan monks.

Turkey Sausage, Cabbage and Apples

1	tablespoon oil
1	pound onions, thinly sliced
1	pound low-fat turkey sausage
¼	teaspoon salt
	Freshly ground pepper
¼	teaspoon crushed red pepper
2	large tart apples (Granny Smith), cored, peeled, thinly sliced
2	tablespoons flour
1	small cabbage (about 1½ pounds), coarsely shredded
½	cup low-sodium chicken broth

Combine the following and set aside:

¼	cup bread crumbs
¾	cup (3 ounces) coarsely grated low-fat sharp Cheddar cheese (preferably white Cheddar)

Preheat oven to 375°. Heat pan and then add olive oil. Sauté onions in the oil until lightly browned; leave in pan. Remove casing from sausage, add to onions. Break up meat in the pan while browning sausage. Stir in salt, pepper and crushed red pepper. Combine apples with flour. In a large casserole dish, spread the cabbage on the bottom of the pan. Next add the apples and then sausage and onions. Pour chicken broth evenly over the top of the pan and sprinkle with cheese topping. Cover tightly with foil and bake 30 minutes or until cooked through and cheese is melted.

Serves: 4-6; Calories: 340; Protein: 28 g; Carbohydrate: 24 g; Total fat: 14 g;
Saturated fat: 3.5 g; Cholesterol: 80 mg; Fiber: 5 g; Sodium: 340 mg

---

*Use a high-quality low-fat sausage. A natural food grocery store,
local Farmer's Market or co-op sells natural meats.
Chicken or pork sausage can be substituted for the turkey.

Asian Beef Stir-Fry
(Bulgogi)

2½   pounds lean rump roast or eye of round roast (have butcher slice ⅛-inch thick or less)

2   tablespoons sherry or white wine

½   tablespoon rice wine vinegar

2   tablespoons sesame oil

½   cup soy sauce

½   cup water

4   tablespoons finely chopped spring onions

2   teaspoons finely grated garlic

1   teaspoon finely grated fresh ginger

1-2   tablespoons sugar

½   teaspoon ground black pepper

2   tablespoons toasted, crushed or whole sesame seeds

Combine the sauce ingredients (all ingredients except the meat) in a large bowl. Add the meat and mix well. Cover and chill overnight, or at least 4 hours. Cook in wok, in a large heavy skillet, or on the grill until meat is done, about 6 to 8 minutes. Serve with Bulgogi Sauce, page 133.

Serves: 8; Calories: 300; Protein: 42 g; Carbohydrate: 4 g; Total fat: 11 g;
Saturated fat: 3 g; Cholesterol: 100 mg; Fiber: 0 g; Sodium: 1115 mg

Market Street Meat Loaf

2	teaspoons vegetable oil
¾	cup finely chopped onion
¼	cup finely chopped celery
2	teaspoons minced garlic
½	teaspoon salt
1½	teaspoons freshly ground black pepper
1	egg and 2 egg whites, beat well
⅓	cup ketchup
⅓	cup evaporated skim milk
1	pound lean ground beef
1	pound lean ground turkey breast
½	cup fine bread crumbs

Sauce:

½	cup ketchup
1	tablespoon Worcestershire sauce
2	tablespoon brown sugar
1	teaspoon mustard

Mix together and spread over meat loaf before baking.

Preheat oven to 375°. Melt the oil in a heavy skillet, and add the onion, celery, and garlic. Cook, stirring often, until the moisture from the vegetables has evaporated, about 10 minutes. Set aside to cool. Combine the salt, black pepper, egg and egg whites in a mixing bowl and beat well. Add the ketchup and evaporated milk. Blend thoroughly. Add the beef, turkey and bread crumbs to the egg mixture. Then add the vegetables and mix thoroughly with your hands, kneading for several minutes. Form the mixture into an oval (resembling a loaf of bread). Place the meat loaf in a baking dish, and place the dish inside a larger pan. Pour boiling water into the larger pan until it reaches halfway up the sides of the baking dish. Place the pan in the oven and bake for 50 to 60 minutes. Remove the baking dish from the water bath and let the meat loaf set for 15 minutes before slicing and serving.

Serves: 10; Calories: 210; Protein: 24 g; Carbohydrate: 15 g; Total fat: 7 g;
Saturated fat: 2 g; Cholesterol: 55 mg; Fiber: 0 g; Sodium: 510 mg

Green Chile Pork Stew
(Guisado de Puerco de Santa Fe)

2½	pounds pork tenderloin
½	cup good red wine
1	cup beer (prefer good lager)
1	teaspoon sugar
2	teaspoons salt
1	tablespoon lime juice
2	tablespoons lemon juice
3	tablespoons extra virgin olive oil
	All-purpose flour
4	cups good quality pork or chicken stock
2	pounds potatoes, peel and quarter lengthwise then in half again
½	pound yellow onions, sliced
2	cups Roma tomatoes, roasted, peeled, and diced
3	cups (1½ pounds cooked) green chiles (Anaheim), roasted, peeled, and diced
12	cloves garlic, minced
	Light sour cream
	Hot corn or flour tortillas

Cut pork into ¾-inch cubes. Mix wine, beer, sugar, salt, lime and lemon juice. Marinate pork in mixture for 3 hours. Drain pork well; set marinade aside. Coat drained pork in flour; seer in medium-hot oil until lightly browned taking care not to burn. Set pork aside. Let pan cool then pour marinade mixture into it and deglaze pan, simmering for a few minutes.

In a stew pot on high, bring stock to a boil then lower flame to maintain a simmer. Pour liquid from pan into stew pot with stock and add tenderloin and onions. Bring to boil, then lower heat and simmer for 5 minutes. Add potatoes then bring to boil, lower heat and simmer until tender, about 10 minutes. Add tomatoes, garlic, and green chiles and bring to a boil; simmer an additional 5 to 10 minutes.

This is best when cooked the day before to allow flavors to blend. Serve with tortillas and top stew with sour cream. For additional garnish, add corn, posole, or sliced zucchini and tomatoes.

Yield: 16 cups; Serves: 8; Calories: 485; Protein: 47 g; Carbohydrate: 40 g; Total fat: 12 g; Saturated fat: 3 g; Cholesterol: 110 mg; Fiber: 6 g; Sodium: 820 mg

Grilled Pork Tenderloin with Red Wine Gastrique

1   **pound pork tenderloin, with visible fat removed**
    Olive oil
    Salt and pepper to taste

Heat a charcoal or gas grill to medium-high. Rub olive oil on the pork and season with salt and pepper. Place meat on grill and cook for about 20 minutes, rotating it several times, until it reaches an internal temperature of 160°. Remove meat from grill and let rest several minutes before slicing.

Red Wine Gastrique:

3   **tablespoons sugar**

4   **tablespoons water**

4   **tablespoons balsamic vinegar**

1-2   **shallots, minced**

1   **cup pinot noir (or red wine of your choice)**

Bring water and sugar to a boil over high heat in a small heavy-bottomed saucepan, stirring until sugar is dissolved. Reduce heat to medium, cover pan with a tight-fitting lid, and simmer for about 4 minutes, until the bubbles forming on the top of the cooking sugar are quarter-sized. Continue cooking until the mixture turns a pale caramel color, about 10 to 15 minutes. Remove from heat and carefully add vinegar, then add shallot and swirl pan over low heat, about 1 minute. Stir in wine and simmer until liquid is reduced to ½ cup, about 10 to 15 minutes. Season with salt and pepper and keep warm, covered until ready to serve.

Serves: 4; Calories:; Protein: 270; Carbohydrate: 15 g; Total fat: 8 g;
Saturated fat: 2.5 g; Cholesterol: 75 mg; Fiber: 0 g; Sodium: 210 mg

Savory Pork with Shiitake Mushrooms

1½   pounds pork tenderloin, sliced ¼-inch thick

    All-purpose flour

2   tablespoons olive oil, divided

2   tablespoons minced garlic

4   ounces fresh shiitake mushrooms, stems removed and caps sliced

¾   cup Marsala wine

¾   cup low-sodium chicken broth

1   large tomato, seeded and chopped

½   cup chopped fresh basil

    Salt and pepper to taste

Working with 1 piece of tenderloin at a time, dip into flour to coat completely. Heat large skillet to medium-high; add olive oil. Add the tenderloin but do not over crowd; lightly brown, about 3 minutes per side. Transfer tenderloin to another dish; cover and set aside. Heat oil over medium-high heat. Add garlic; sauté 1 minute. Add mushrooms; cook 2 minutes. Add Marsala wine, broth, and tomato to the pan. Simmer until slightly thickened, about 6 minutes. Stir in basil. Season with salt and pepper to taste. Add cooked tenderloin to sauce and simmer for 5 more minutes.

Serves: 6; Calories: 250; Protein: 34 g; Carbohydrate: 5 g; Total fat: 8 g;
Saturated fat: 3 g; Cholesterol: 95 mg; Fiber: 1 g; Sodium: 90 mg

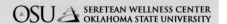

Southern Pulled Pork Tenderloin

1	tablespoon olive oil
1	medium onion, chopped
1	garlic clove, minced
2	tablespoons cider vinegar
¼	cup ketchup
2	tablespoons ketchup style chili sauce
2	teaspoons Worcestershire sauce
1	teaspoon Tabasco sauce
¾	cup water
½	teaspoon salt
¼	teaspoon fresh ground pepper
1	(¾-pound) pork tenderloin, halved crosswise

Heat oil in 4-quart heavy saucepan over moderate heat. Add onion and garlic and cook, stirring, until golden, about 8 minutes. Stir in remaining ingredients, bring to simmer and cook covered, for 10 minutes.

Add pork, cover and simmer, turning occasionally until tender, about 45 minutes.

Transfer pork to cutting board. Purée cooking liquid in a blender until smooth (use caution) and return to pan. When pork is cool enough to handle, shred with your fingers or two forks. Add pork back to the sauce and simmer, stirring, just until pork is heated through. The shredded pork in sauce can be made up to 1 day ahead and refrigerated, covered. Serve on soft buns.

Serves: 6; Calories: 170; Protein: 22 g; Carbohydrate: 7 g; Total fat: 6 g;
Saturated fat: 1.5 g; Cholesterol: 60 mg; Fiber: 0 g; Sodium: 540 mg

Orange and black are OSU's colors because the first
athletic teams were called the "Tigers" –after the Princeton Tigers.

Marinated Pork Tenderloin

For the marinade:

3	ounces balsamic vinegar
3	ounces light soy sauce
1	tablespoon olive oil
½	teaspoon dried thyme
1	teaspoon fresh minced garlic
½	teaspoon dried red pepper flakes
	Black pepper to taste
2	(1 pound) pork tenderloins, fat removed
	Olive oil

Combine marinade ingredients and place in shallow baking dish. Add meat, turning to coat, then cover with plastic and marinate in refrigerator for several hours.

Heat a grill pan or large skillet on medium high heat to very hot. Remove meat from marinade. Spray pan lightly and place pork in pan. Cook for several minutes on each side until lightly browned. Transfer pork to the oven and roast for 15 to 20 minutes or until desired tenderness. Let rest for 10 minutes before serving. Slice the pork into ¼-inch slices and serve.

Serves: 6; Calories: 210; Protein: 32 g; Carbohydrate: 0 g; Total fat: 7 g;
Saturated fat: 2 g; Cholesterol: 100 mg; Fiber: 0 g; Sodium: 200 mg

This marinade recipe also works well with chicken breasts.

Golden Baked Cod

1	pound fresh cod fillet
1	egg, lightly beaten
⅔	cup plain breadcrumbs
1	tablespoon olive oil
	Salt and pepper to taste
	Lemon wedges

Rinse and pat dry the fish with a paper towel; set aside. In two separate bowls, put the egg and breadcrumbs. First roll the fish in the egg and then the breadcrumbs until evenly coated. Lightly salt and pepper fish.

Preheat oven to 400°. Heat a skillet on medium high; add the olive oil. Lightly brown the fish for 1 to 2 minutes per side. Place the fish on a baking sheet and put in the preheated oven for 5 more minutes or until fish flakes easily. Serve with lemon wedges.

Serves: 4; Calories: 220; Protein: 24 g; Carbohydrate: 13 g; Total fat: 7 g; Saturated fat: 1 g; Cholesterol: 100 mg; Fiber: 0 g; Sodium: 330 mg

An OSU graduate invented the personal computer.

Grilled Salmon Burgers

¾   **pound skinless salmon fillet, finely diced by hand**

3   **tablespoons low-fat mayonnaise**

1½   **tablespoons chopped fresh dill**

¼   **teaspoon salt**

⅛   **teaspoon fresh ground pepper**

1   **small garlic clove, minced**

2   **tablespoons dry breadcrumbs**

2   **rolls, split and toasted**

2   **tablespoons tartar sauce or cole slaw, optional**

     Lettuce and tomato slices

Place chopped salmon fillet, 3 tablespoons low-fat mayonnaise, 2 tablespoons dill, salt, garlic, and pepper in a bowl. Mix well and form into two patties. They can be prepared and refrigerated up to 6 hours ahead.

Prepare grill for medium-high heat. Spray a grill rack with vegetable oil. Grill salmon until fish is cooked through, about 8 minutes total. Cooking time depends on the heat of the grill and thickness of the salmon. It is easier to flip the burgers if you grill the first side for 5 minutes before turning. Toast rolls and spread with tartar sauce or cole slaw before serving.

To cook on the stove top, use a lightly oiled preheated grill pan over medium-high heat.

Serves: 2; Calories: 400; Protein: 33 g; Carbohydrate: 34 g; Total fat: 14 g;
Saturated fat: 2 g; Cholesterol: 80 mg; Fiber: 1 g; Sodium: 600 mg

*To skin salmon, put the tip of a sharp knife just under the skin.
Slowly cut along fillet to remove the skin. If you ask, the butcher will remove the skin for you.*

* Do not use a food processor, it ruins the texture of the burger.*

Herb Marinated Swordfish

¼   **cup lemon juice**

3   **tablespoons olive oil**

1   **tablespoon fresh herbs (rosemary leaves, oregano or thyme), chopped**

1   **garlic clove, minced**

¼   **teaspoon salt**

     Fresh ground black pepper, to taste

4   **swordfish steaks, ¾-inch thick (about 6 ounces each)**

     Fresh lemon wedges for garnish

Whisk together lemon juice, oil, rosemary, garlic, salt, and pepper in small bowl. Place fish in shallow glass pan or a zip-lock plastic bag; pour marinade over fish and leave for 30 minutes or up to 1 hour in refrigerator. Bring to room temperature before grilling.

Prepare grill and when ready, put fish on grill rack. Do not let too much of the marinade drip into the fire, as it may cause fire to flare. After the first 5 minutes carefully flip fish over with a spatula and cook another 5 minutes. The length of time will depend on the heat of the grill and thickness of fish. Total cooking time will be around 10 minutes. Check for doneness by cutting into thickest part of fish with the tip of knife (or 140 degrees on meat thermometer). The fish is done when it changes color from translucent to opaque. Garnish fish with lemon wedge and sprig of fresh herbs. Other herbs may be substituted for rosemary, such as thyme, dill, basil, and parsley.

Alternative method of cooking: Preheat oven to 425°. Heat a heavy pan on stove until hot; add fish and let it brown on each side for 1 to 2 minutes. Place fish on heavy baking pan and roast until the center turns from translucent to opaque, 8 to 10 minutes.

Serving: 6 ounces; Calories: 265; Protein: 43 g; Carbohydrate: 0 g; Total fat: 8 g;
Saturated fat: 5 g; Cholesterol: 85 mg; Fiber: 0 g; Sodium: 195 mg

---

Tuna or salmon may be substituted for the swordfish.

Mexican Red Snapper

4	(6 ounces each), red snapper fillets, or any favorite mild white fish
3	tablespoons lime juice
2	teaspoons cumin
½	teaspoon cinnamon
2	tablespoons olive oil, divided
1	medium onion, thinly sliced
4	garlic cloves, sliced thin
1	(15-ounce) can unsalted tomatoes
1	bunch cilantro, chopped

Marinate the fish in lime juice, cumin, cinnamon, and 1 tablespoon olive oil for 20 minutes or up to 1 hour.

In large sauté pan, heat the oil; add onions and fish and sauté for about 5 minutes. Remove fish to a baking dish set aside. Add the garlic and sauté briefly; deglaze the pan with tomatoes. Simmer for 5 minutes then add the fish back into the pan. Add cilantro and coat fish with sauce. Carefully remove fish to serving dish and top with remaining sauce.

Serves: 4; Calories: 270; Protein: 35 g; Carbohydrate: 12 g; Total fat: 9 g;
Saturated fat: 1 g; Cholesterol: 65 mg; Fiber: 3 g; Sodium: 110 mg

*To prevent food from sticking in sauté pan, make sure your
pan is hot before adding any oil. In other words, hot pan, cold oil and food won't stick!*

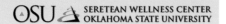
New Mexico Style Shrimp Burrito

1	cucumber, peeled, seeded, and diced
¼	cup diced onion
½	cup chopped fresh cilantro
1	fresh serrano chile, seeded, and finely minced
1	small ripe mango, peeled and diced
2	teaspoons olive oil
3	teaspoons red wine vinegar
	Pinch of salt
1½	pounds large shrimp, peeled and deveined
2	tablespoons olive oil
1	tablespoon ground red chile powder (New Mexico chiles preferred)
1	cup black beans, cooked and drained
½	cup (3 ounces) goat cheese or feta cheese
8	flour tortillas

To prepare the salsa, in a medium bowl mix together the cucumber, onion, cilantro, serrano chile, mango, olive oil, vinegar, and salt. This may be done several hours before serving.

Peel shrimp and mix together with 2 tablespoons olive oil and 1 tablespoon Chimayo chile powder. This may be prepared several hours before serving. In a small bowl, mash goat cheese with a fork and let it come to room temperature before making burrito.

Prepare charcoal grill. When coals are hot, place shrimp on grill rack about 2 to 3 minutes per side, turning once. Heat black beans in small saucepan until hot. Heat skillet over high heat. Add tortillas, one at a time, and heat for 15 seconds per side. Keep tortillas warm by wrapping them in a dry cloth towel. To assemble burrito, place tortilla on a warmed plate. Spread 1 tablespoon goat cheese on tortilla, add 2 tablespoons black beans, 4-5 grilled shrimp, 2-3 tablespoons cucumber salsa. Fold tortilla and place on serving plate.

Yield: 8; Calories: 330; Protein: 25 g; Carbohydrate: 31 g; Total fat: 11 g;
Saturated fat: 3 g; Cholesterol: 175 mg; Fiber: 4 g; Sodium: 415 gm

---

Salmon with Fresh Herbs

2	pounds salmon
½	teaspoon salt, divided
½	tablespoon butter
1	tablespoon olive oil
½	cup cilantro, chopped
3	cloves garlic, chopped
¼	cup dried barberries, cleaned and washed
¼	teaspoon freshly ground black pepper
	Parsley and green onions, chopped
	Lemon slices

Preheat oven to 375°. Wash fish and pat dry. Remove any bones with tweezers. Rub the fish with ½ tablespoon butter, ¼ teaspoon salt, and 1 clove of crushed garlic. Arrange the fish in a large pan sprayed with vegetable oil. Place the fish in the oven and bake for 30 minutes or until the fish flakes easily with a fork.

While the fish is cooking, heat the olive oil in a skillet and sauté 2 garlic cloves for several minutes. Add the cilantro, barberries, ¼ teaspoon salt, and pepper. Mix well. When the fish is almost done, spread the cilantro and garlic mixture over the fish. Bake the salmon an additional 5 minutes. Arrange fish on a serving platter and garnish with chopped parsley, green onions, and lemon slices. Serve with saffron rice.

Note: If dried barberries are used, they must be soaked in a bowl of cold water for 10 minutes. Lift out carefully, rinse and drain. Dried barberries are available in Middle Eastern food specialty stores. If unavailable, substitute chopped dried blueberries or cranberries.

Serves: 6; Calories: 330; Protein: 40 g; Carbohydrate: 3 g; Total fat: 16 g;
Saturated fat: 2.5 g; Cholesterol: 95 mg; Fiber: 0 g; Sodium: 290 mg

*If wild salmon is available, it has the lowest fat content. All salmon is a good source of omega 3 fats.
To reduce your risk of heart disease, aim for 2 to 3 servings of fish per week.

*Halibut fillets work well with this recipe too.

Sesame Crusted Salmon with Red Pepper Coulis

4   **(6-ounce) portions of salmon, skin removed**

¼   **cup hulled raw sesame seeds**

      Pinch salt

1   **tablespoon olive oil**

Dredge the salmon portions in the sesame seeds. In a large oven proof sauté pan, heat the olive oil. Lightly brown the salmon on each side. Place in 400 degree oven for approximately 8 minutes —just until salmon is done. Sprinkle with sea salt if desired. Serve salmon with the Red Pepper Coulis Sauce, page 135.

Serves: 4; Calories: 290; Carbohydrate: 5 g; Protein: 31 g; Total fat: 15 g; Saturated fat: 2.5 g; Cholesterol: 80 mg; Fiber: 2 g; Sodium: 450 mg

Oklahoma State is such a great place that ESPN chose the campus for the debut of the network's new 24-hour college sports network called ESPNU. The new network debuted in March 2005 with a two-hour live special edition ESPNU College GameDay and a pep rally and free concert in Gallagher-Iba Arena.

Adriatic Style Shrimp Brochettes

1½	pounds large shrimp, peeled and deveined
3½	tablespoons olive oil
3½	tablespoons canola oil
⅔	cup fine, dry unflavored bread crumbs
2	teaspoons minced garlic
2	teaspoons minced parsley
¾	teaspoon salt
	Black pepper to taste
	Lemon wedges

Prepare grill or preheat broiler. Put shrimp in large bowl. Add the oil and bread crumbs to the shrimp and mix lightly to get an even coating on all the shrimp. Add the garlic, parsley, salt, and pepper and mix well. Allow the shrimp to set for 20 minutes at room temperature.

Skewer the shrimp lengthwise in two places, using 3 to 5 shrimp per skewer. Cook the shrimp for 3 minutes on one side and 2 minutes on the other over hot coals or broil. Make sure the temperature is very hot so the shrimp can cook quickly. Each side is done as soon as a crisp, golden crust forms. Serve hot with lemon wedges on the side.

Serves: 6; Calories: 250; Protein: 25 g; Carbohydrate: 10 g; Total fat: 12 g;
Saturated fat: 1.5 g; Cholesterol: 170 mg; Fiber: 0 g; Sodium: 450 mg

Spicy Grilled Shrimp

2	pounds large shrimp, peeled and deveined
1	tablespoon reduced-sodium soy sauce
2	tablespoons dry sherry
2	tablespoons minced garlic
1	tablespoon minced fresh gingerroot
1	tablespoon sesame oil
1	tablespoon canola oil
1½	teaspoons sugar
½	teaspoon ground red cayenne pepper

Mix all marinade ingredients together in a large glass bowl. Add shrimp and marinate in the refrigerator at least 1 hour, stirring shrimp occasionally. Remove from refrigerator 15 minutes before grilling. Prepare a charcoal grill. When coals are medium-hot, grill shrimp for 3 minutes per side or until curled and pink (use a perforated grill rack or skewer shrimp).

Serves: 6; Calories: 215; Protein: 31 g; Carbohydrate: 4 g; Total fat: 7 g;
Saturated fat: 1 g; Cholesterol: 230 mg; Fiber: 0 g; Sodium: 325 mg

Cimarron Review

Since 1967, Cimarron Review has published authors such as Nobel Prize winner Jose Saramago, Rick Moody, Robert Olen Butler, Jonathan Ames, Mark Doty, Diane Wakoski, Tess Gallagher, Richard Shelton, Mark Halliday, Jerome Rothenberg, Nin Andrews, and many others. This past year, Writers Digest *included us in its top fifty places to publish fiction in America, and* Esquire *has called Cimarron "one of America's literary roots."*

Linguine alla Cecca

Pizza alla Napolitana

1	recipe Hard Pizza Dough, page 77
1	teaspoon olive oil
6	ounces Pizza Sauce, page 137
1	can flat anchovy filets
½	bunch fresh oregano leaves, chopped
12	ounces fresh mozzarella, sliced
¼	cup Parmesan, grated

Preheat oven and pizza stone to 450°. Roll pizza dough out to 14 inches.

Rub dough all over with olive oil. Top with pizza sauce. Sprinkle the oregano liberally over the pizza. Chop up or leave the anchovies whole and spread evenly over the dough; top with the mozzarella and Parmesan cheese. Place on the pizza stone in a preheated oven and bake for 8 to 10 minutes.

Serves: 8 pieces; Calories: 420; Protein: 26 g; Carbohydrate: 45 g; Total fat: 13 g; Saturated fat: 6 g; Cholesterol: 35 mg; Fiber: 5 g; Sodium: 680 mg

OSU's Residential Life programs have won more national awards for student programming, including school of the year three times, than any other residential life program in the nation.

Pizza alla Norma

1	recipe Basic Whole Wheat Dough, page 76
1	eggplant sliced thin crosswise
2	(14-ounce) cans unsalted tomatoes in juice
½	bunch mint leaves, whole
10	ounces fresh ricotta cheese
3	ounces grated Parmesan
1	tablespoon olive oil
¼	teaspoon kosher salt

Lightly brush both sides of eggplant with olive oil. Place on sheet pan and lightly sprinkle with salt. Roast in 350° oven until eggplant turns a very light golden color. Let cool until ready to use.

Drain half of the juice of the tomatoes; crush the tomatoes roughly.

Roll out your dough; brush with oil. Spread tomatoes with a little juice on the crust, then spread out the mint, arrange eggplant and top with ricotta and Parmesan cheese. Bake on a pizza stone in a 450° oven until very dark golden brown.

Serves: 8; Calories: 320; Protein: 17 g; Carbohydrate: 45 g; Total fat: 11 g;
Saturated fat: 3.5 g; Cholesterol: 20 mg; Fiber: 8 g; Sodium: 480 mg

Basic Whole Wheat Dough

¼   cup warm water

1   teaspoon honey

1   tablespoon dry yeast

1   cup cold water

2   tablespoons olive oil

3   cups whole wheat flour

1   teaspoon kosher salt

Blend ¼ cup of warm water with the yeast and honey let it get nice and foamy (about 10 minutes). In large mixing bowl combine flour, salt, oil, and the remainder of the water (don't mix yet). When yeast is ready, add it to the flour mixture and knead until smooth and soft. You can do this with an electric mixer with the dough paddle attachment or by hand.

Once you are finished kneading the dough, divide the dough in half and roll into nice smooth balls. Place on a plate or in a pie tin and cover with a towel. Let dough rise to double in size. This may take up to one hour at room temperature. When dough is ready, roll it out for pizza.

Yield: 2 (14-inch) pizzas

*Faculty in Human Environmental Sciences and Psychology submitted a proposal
for an intervention program to help decrease child obesity. The proposal was approved for
funding of $1 million by the U.S. Department of Agriculture. The goal is to decrease child obesity, while
improving children's level of psychological and social functioning. The U.S.D.A.
rated OSU's proposal as number one in the nation.*

Hard Pizza Dough
(Thin Crunchy Cracker Like Crusts)

¼	cup warm water
1	tablespoon honey
1	tablespoon dry yeast
1	cup cold water
2	tablespoons olive oil
1½	cups whole wheat flour
1½	cups semolina flour
1	teaspoon kosher salt

Blend ¼ cup of warm water with the yeast and honey; let it get nice and foamy (about 10 minutes). In a large mixing bowl, combine flour, salt, oil, and the remainder of the water (don't mix yet). When yeast is ready, add it to the flour mixture and knead until smooth and soft. You can do this with an electric mixer with the dough paddle attachment or by hand. Once you are finished kneading the dough, place it in a lightly oiled bowl, cover and let rise to double in size. This may take up to one hour at room temperature. When dough is ready, divide into half and roll into nice smooth balls. Place on a plate or in a pie tin and cover with a towel to rise double in size again. After that you're ready to roll it out for pizza.

Yield: 2 (14-inch) pizzas

Baked Rigatoni with Tomatoes and Cheese

2	tablespoons olive oil
3	garlic cloves, minced
6	(15-ounce) cans no-salt tomatoes, drained and crushed
1	teaspoon dried basil
2	cups reduced sodium chicken broth
½	teaspoon crushed red pepper
1	cup (¾ ounce) fresh basil, chopped
1	pound rigatoni or penne pasta
8	ounces Havarti or fresh mozzarella cheese, grated
⅓	cup Parmesan cheese, grated

Heat olive oil in heavy large Dutch oven over medium-high heat. Add garlic; sauté about 5 minutes. Mix in tomatoes, dried basil, chicken broth, and crushed red pepper. Bring to a simmer, uncovered, stirring occasionally, until mixture thickens (about 1 hour). Stir in chopped fresh basil. Preheat oven to 375°. Cook pasta in large pot until tender but still firm to bite. Drain well. Return pasta to same pot. Pour sauce over pasta and toss to blend. Mix in Havarti or mozzarella cheese. Transfer to a large glass baking dish. Spread Parmesan evenly over top. Bake 30 minutes or until pasta is heated through.

Serves: 10; Calories: 375; Protein: 15 g; Carbohydrate: 41 g; Total fat: 14 g; Saturated fat: 1 g; Cholesterol: 80 mg; Fiber 3 g; Sodium 780 mg

OSU is the home of 45 NCAA championships plus one national championship in women's equestrian. More than 140 OSU athletes have been crowned individual national champions.

Fusilli with Pesto and Sautéed Chicken

2	garlic cloves
1½	cups fresh basil leaves
¼	cup pine nuts (may substitute walnuts or pecans)
¼	cup extra virgin olive oil
¼	cup Parmesan cheese, grated
	Salt to taste
8	ounces dried fusilli (or your favorite pasta)
1	tablespoon olive oil
1	pound boneless, skinless chicken breast

Wash basil leaves (just before using), dry, and remove large parts of stems. In a food processor, chop garlic, add basil and chop, and then add nuts and process. With food processor running, slowly add olive oil, next add Parmesan cheese. Add salt to taste. Add more oil or water, if desired, to thin the consistency of sauce. Purée until pesto is smooth and creamy. Pesto may be frozen. Put in a plastic container, spread a light layer of olive oil over pesto and cover the container (keep airtight to retain light green, fresh color).

Bring a pot of water to a boil. Add pasta, and cook until tender but still slightly firm to the bite. While pasta is cooking; cut chicken into 1-inch cubes. Heat olive oil in a skillet or wok; add chicken and sauté to lightly brown it. Place cooked chicken in deep bowl. Place drained pasta in bowl with chicken and toss together with pesto. Serve with grated fresh Parmesan cheese.

Serves: 4; Calories: 550; Protein: 37 g; Carbohydrate: 42 g; Total fat: 26 g;
Saturated fat: 4.5 g; Cholesterol: 70 mg; Fiber: 3 g; Sodium: 170 mg

*When fresh basil is available in your garden or at the farmer's market,
whip up some pesto to make a delicious entrée.

Gemelli Pasta with Sausage and Tomatoes

1	pound turkey sausage
3	tablespoons olive oil
3	leeks, white part only, rinsed well, quartered and diced (or small onion)
4	garlic cloves, minced
¼	teaspoon crushed red pepper
½	cup chicken stock, low-sodium
1	(14-ounce) can unsalted tomatoes, drained, seeded, and chopped
¼	cup fresh parsley, chopped
	Salt and pepper to taste
½	pound gemelli pasta, or any shape of your choice
½	cup Parmesan cheese, grated

Remove casing from turkey sausage and slice into pieces. Heat 2 tablespoons olive oil in a large saucepan; add sausage and sauté for about 5 minutes breaking it up with a fork as it cooks. When it is half cooked, add the leeks, garlic, and crushed red pepper and continue cooking until the leeks are soft and the sausage is cooked through about another 5 minutes. Add a tablespoon of chicken stock if needed to prevent sticking. Pour in all of the chicken stock, tomatoes, parsley, and 1 tablespoon of olive oil. Continue to cook an additional 5 to 10 minutes. Season with salt and pepper if desired.

While sauce is cooking, bring a large pot of water to a boil. Add the pasta and cook uncovered according to package instructions. Be sure you do not overcook the pasta. When it is ready, drain immediately and add the pasta into the finished sauce. Serve with grated cheese.

Serves: 4; Calories: 490; Protein: 32 g; Carbohydrate: 47 g; Total fat: 24 g; Saturated fat: 6 g; Cholesterol: 55 mg; Fiber: 4 g; Sodium: 920 mg

You can substitute other pasta shapes such as shells, wagon wheels, or spirals.

Use any high-quality natural turkey, chicken, or pork sausage.

Homemade Macaroni and Cheese

8	ounces pasta shells
1½	cups cottage cheese (not fat-free)
1	cup skim milk, divided
1	tablespoon white flour
1	cup (4 ounces) sharp low-fat Cheddar cheese, grated
¼	teaspoon salt
¼	teaspoon pepper
3	tablespoons Parmesan cheese, grated
2	tablespoons fine dry bread crumbs
1	teaspoon olive oil

Preheat oven to 350°. Put large pot of water on stove and bring to a boil. Add noodles to the boiling water and cook for 8 to 10 minutes. Carefully pour noodles and water into a colander and rinse under cold water. Set noodles aside. While noodles are boiling, purée cottage cheese in a blender or food processor until smooth.

Stir 1 tablespoon flour into ¼ cup cold milk and whisk until smooth. Heat ¾ cup milk in saucepan. Add flour and milk mixture to hot milk. Continue to stir for several minutes or until slightly thick. Remove from heat and stir in the grated Cheddar cheese. When it has melted, stir in cottage cheese, salt and pepper. Stir in the cooked pasta shells. Spoon into a glass baking dish. Mix Parmesan, bread crumbs, and olive oil together and sprinkle over the pasta. Cover and bake for 15 minutes; uncover and bake an additional 5 to 10 minutes.

Serves: 4; Calories: 380; Protein: 30 g; Carbohydrate: 50 g; Total fat: 7 g;
Saturated fat: 4 g; Cholesterol: 25 mg; Fiber: 1.5 g; Sodium: 750 mg

*Comfort food for many, this version provides an added bonus of
extra protein, calcium, and less sodium than the box variety.*

Mediterranean Pasta Salad

1	pound penne pasta or desired shape (white or whole wheat)
2	medium zucchinis cut into 1-inch half moons
1	medium eggplant, cut into 1-inch cubes
8	ounces mushrooms, halved or quartered depending on size
1	tablespoon olive oil
1	red bell pepper, roasted
2	Roma tomatoes, seeded and diced
5	ounces feta cheese, crumbled

Sun-Dried Tomato Vinaigrette:

⅓	cup sun-dried tomatoes
¼	cup red wine vinegar
2	garlic cloves
¼	cup fresh parsley
½	cup fresh basil
	Pinch of cayenne pepper
⅓	cup olive oil
	Salt and pepper to taste

Preheat oven to 400°. Cook the pasta according to package instructions; drain and run under cold water to cool. Place cut zucchini, eggplant, and mushrooms on a sheet pan lined with parchment to prevent sticking. Drizzle vegetables with olive oil. Place in oven and roast until lightly brown about 30 minutes. Roast red pepper under broiler, turning periodically, until blackened on all sides. Place in a plastic bag for 10-15 minutes; when cool enough to handle, peel off skin, remove seeds, and then dice. Combine pasta and vegetables.

(continued)

Mediterranean Pasta Salad *(continued)*

Reconstitute tomatoes by placing in a small bowl and cover with boiling water; let sit about 15 minutes until soft and drain. Place tomatoes, vinegar, garlic, herbs, and cayenne into the bowl of a food processor or kitchen blender and process to combine. Slowly drizzle in oil while machine is running. Season with salt and pepper. Pour dressing over pasta and vegetables; stir until dressing covers all the ingredients. It is best to add the salad dressing when you are ready to serve. Top with diced tomatoes and feta cheese.

Serves: 8; Calories: 410; Protein: 20 g; Carbohydrate: 50 g; Total fat: 15 g; Saturated fat: 4 g; Cholesterol: 100 mg; Fiber: 4 g; Sodium: 330 mg

*Whole wheat pasta provides additional fiber, and can be substituted for pasta made with white semolina flour.

Linguine alla Cecca

5   large fresh tomatoes
⅓   cup olive oil
2   garlic cloves, sliced in half
1   cup fresh basil, chopped
    Crushed red pepper, to taste
1   pound linguine

Drop 5 large tomatoes into boiling water for 1 full minute. Let cool slightly and peel, seed, and chop the tomatoes. Put them into a large bowl with ⅓ cup of olive oil, 2 garlic cloves sliced in half, the basil, and crushed red pepper.

Refrigerate the tomatoes for a couple of hours; remove the garlic before serving. Boil 1 pound of linguine, drain and toss with the cold tomato mixture. Serve immediately.

Serves: 6; Calories: 425; Protein: 12 g; Carbohydrate: 56 g; Total fat: 16 g; Saturated fat: 2 g; Cholesterol: 85 mg; Fiber: 2.5 g; Sodium: 25 mg

This recipe is best when home-grown tomatoes are available.

Penne with Roasted Peppers, Eggplant and Zucchini

1	red and 1 yellow bell pepper cut into ½-inch strips
1	pound eggplant cut into ¾-inch thick dice
1½	pounds zucchini cut in half lengthwise and across in ½-inch slices
3	tablespoons olive oil
1½	teaspoons black pepper
1	pound dried penne pasta (or any shape)
4	cups Tomato Sauce, page 137
1	pound mozzarella cheese, shredded
1	cup Parmesan cheese

Preheat oven to 400°. Toss vegetables with olive oil. Spread vegetables on two large sheet pans. Roast for 30 minutes in preheated oven, stirring occasionally. Season with pepper and set aside.

Bring a pot of water to a boil. Add pasta and stir frequently. Boil about 10 minutes or until slightly firm to the bite. Drain and let cool slightly.

Lightly coat the bottom of a 9 x 13-inch baking pan with tomato sauce. In a large bowl, add pasta, vegetables, tomato sauce, mozzarella, and half of the Parmesan cheese. Transfer the mixture to the baking dish (this can be made a day ahead and refrigerated until ready to bake). About 1 hour before serving, preheat oven to 375°. Sprinkle with remaining Parmesan. Bake covered with foil for 30 minutes; uncover and bake for 10 or 15 minutes more or until hot and cheese has melted.

Serves: 10; Calories: 455; Protein: 24 g; Carbohydrate: 48 g; Total fat: 18 g; Saturated fat: 7 g; Cholesterol: 85 mg; Fiber: 6 g; Sodium: 640 mg

Roasted Cherry Tomato Sauce with Orecchiette

For the sauce:

2½   pounds cherry tomatoes, halved

¼   cup olive oil

5   garlic cloves, minced

1   tablespoon balsamic vinegar

¼   teaspoon crushed red pepper

¼   cup fresh basil, chopped

For the pasta:

¾   pound orecchiette (or pasta of your choice)

¼   cup Kalamata olives, chopped pitted

6   ounces feta cheese, crumbled (about 1 cup)

3   tablespoons pine nuts, lightly toasted

       Optional: ¾ pound grilled chicken breasts, sliced or 1 pound grilled shrimp

Position rack in center of oven and preheat to 375°. Combine tomatoes, oil, garlic, vinegar and red pepper in roasting pan or 13 x 9-inch glass baking dish. Roast until tomatoes are tender, stirring occasionally, about 45 minutes. Stir in basil.

Cook pasta in large pot of boiling water until just tender but still firm to the bite. Drain. Return to pot. Add tomatoes and olives. Stir over low heat until heated through, about 2 to 3 minutes. Add feta cheese and stir until melted and creamy, about 2 minutes. Divide pasta among 4 plates; sprinkle with pine nuts and chicken or shrimp if desired.

Serves: 6; Calories: 530; Protein: 31 g; Carbohydrate: 54 g; Total fat: 20 g;
Saturated fat: 6 g; Cholesterol: 70 mg; Fiber: 4 g; Sodium: 430 mg

*Cooked tomatoes are high in lycopene, a carotenoid that protects against cancer.

Sesame Noodle Salad

1	pound linguine noodles, broken in half
1	teaspoon canola or light olive oil
1	red bell pepper, thinly sliced
8	asparagus spears, sliced on the diagonal
4	green onions, thinly sliced
	Toasted sesame seeds to garnish

Cook the pasta according to package instructions. Drain and run under cold water to cool. Toss the pasta with a small amount of vegetable oil to prevent sticking.

Cook the asparagus for about 1 minute in boiling water. Drain and run under cold water.

Combine the pasta, red pepper, asparagus and scallions.

Sesame Dressing:

2	tablespoons rice vinegar		1	tablespoon fresh ginger, peeled and chopped
3	tablespoons light soy sauce			
1	tablespoon brown sugar		⅓	cup canola or light olive oil
2	teaspoons Dijon mustard		1½	tablespoons sesame oil
2	tablespoons fresh squeezed lime juice		½	teaspoon cayenne, more or less to taste
2	garlic cloves, chopped			Salt and pepper to taste

In a blender, add the vinegar, soy sauce, mustard, lime juice, brown sugar, garlic and ginger. Process well. Combine oils and, with blender running, slowly drizzle them in so that the dressing comes together or emulsifies. Season with cayenne, and the salt and pepper. Pour dressing over salad and combine. Garnish with the sesame seeds.

Serves: 8; Calories: 310; Protein: 10 g; Carbohydrate: 46 g; Total fat: 10 g;
Saturated fat: 1 g; Cholesterol: 0 mg; Fiber: 3 g; Sodium: 190 mg

---

Basic Egg Pasta
(Using Stand Mixer)

2   **large eggs**
1   **extra large egg**
2   **tablespoons water**
2¾   **cups sifted all-purpose, unbleached flour**

Break eggs into a glass measuring cup and add water. Add additional water to make a combined liquid of ¾ cup. Sift flour into bowl, and with a flat beater on speed 2, gradually add egg and water mixture. Mix for 30 seconds or until completely integrated.

Exchange flat beater for dough hook. Ball the dough into the center. Knead on speed 2 for 2 minutes. Hand knead for 30 to 60 seconds. Without a dough hook, hand knead for 4 to 5 minutes. Cover dough with plastic wrap and refrigerate for no less than 15 minutes and no more than 4 hours.

Extrude through pasta attachment or roll flat and cut. Separate noodles. Cook in boiling water. Flat noodles take about 10 minutes to cook, but it will depend on thickness and desired tenderness. Serve immediately. Store cooked noodles in refrigerator for up to 3 days. Add 1 tablespoon oil per pound of cooked pasta to keep in the refrigerator. Serve with Italian Tomato Sauce, page 138.

Yield: 1 pound pasta; Serves: 6; Calories: 260; Protein: 10 g; Carbohydrate: 45 g; Total fat: 3 g; Saturated fat: < 1 g; Cholesterol: 105 mg; Fiber: 0 g; Sodium: 55 mg

Papyrus

Papyrus is OSU's undergraduate literary journal. Founded in 1995, it was a continuation of an earlier journal called Soliloquy. Papyrus is an outlet for OSU undergraduate students to publish their art, short fiction, and poetry. Publications are annual, and come out at the end of the spring semester.

talian-Style Zucchini

Avocado and Grapefruit Salad

2	avocados, ripe but firm, halved and pitted
2	grapefruits, segmented, with juice
¼	red onion, finely sliced
2	tablespoons extra-virgin olive oil
½	teaspoon sea salt
1	bunch arugula, spinach, or watercress, cleaned and stemmed
	Parmesan cheese, shaved

Scoop avocado from skins and cut into thin slices. In bowl, combine avocado, grapefruit with juice, onion, olive oil, and salt.

On salad plate, make small bed of arugula, spinach, or watercress; spoon avocado mixture on top. Garnish with a few shavings of Parmesan cheese.

Serves: 4; Calories: 290; Protein: 4 g; Carbohydrate: 24 g; Total fat: 19 g; Saturated fat: 3 g; Cholesterol: 0 mg; Fiber: 14 g; Sodium: 290 mg

Dark greens provide an abundance of folic acid which can prevent birth defects and promote heart health by lowering homocysteine levels.

Beet Salad with Oranges and Walnuts

1	large bunch beets, 2 pounds
3	large oranges
1½	tablespoons olive oil
1½	teaspoons balsamic vinegar
1	garlic clove, minced
¼	teaspoon Dijon mustard
½	red onion (½ cup), sliced and quartered
⅓	cup walnut pieces, toasted and broken
	Boston or leaf lettuce

Cut stems from beets to within 1-inch. Simmer beets in boiling water for 50 minutes or until tender. Pierce with a fork and when ready rinse in cold water to remove skin. Trim off stem, rinse, and drain the beets. Chop beets into bite-size pieces and chill separately in covered bowl. Peel oranges with a knife and slice in sections removing membrane. Put oranges in a small bowl and refrigerate until ready to assemble salad.

In a small dish, whisk together olive oil, vinegar, garlic, and mustard. In large salad bowl, gently combine the beets, oranges, onions, walnuts, and dressing. Chill for an hour or more before serving. Serve ½ cup portion on lettuce leaf.

Serves: 8; Calories: 120; Protein: 5 g; Carbohydrate: 17 g; Total fat: 6 g; Saturated fat: .5 g; Cholesterol: 0 g; Fiber: 4 g; Sodium: 45 mg

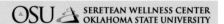
Cucumber, Tomato, and Avocado Salad

3   **small cucumbers, peeled and seeded**

3   **ripe tomatoes, diced**

2   **ripe avocados, diced**

2   **tablespoons red onion, slivered**

¼   **cup olive oil**

2   **tablespoons white balsamic vinegar**

2   **garlic cloves, minced**

¼   **cup cilantro, chopped or to taste**

    Salt and pepper to taste

Cut cucumber in half lengthwise and slice crosswise into crescents. In a serving bowl, combine cucumber, tomato, avocado, and red onion. In a blender, combine olive oil, garlic, vinegar, and cilantro. Mix briefly and pour over salad. Salt and pepper to taste.

Serves: 8; Calories: 160; Protein: 2 g; Carbohydrate: 9 g; Total fat: 14 g;
Saturated fat: 2.5 g; Cholesterol: 0 mg; Fiber: 5 g; Sodium: 10 mg

This salad is best when using fresh picked tomatoes.

Fall Greens with Tarragon Vinaigrette and Gorgonzola Croutons

Gorgonzola Croutons:

3   ounces firm Gorgonzola cheese cut into 1-inch squares, freeze for 30 minutes

In three small bowls set aside the following:

½   cup flour

1   whipped egg

½   cup unseasoned bread crumbs

Lightly toss Gorgonzola cubes in flour. Shake off excess. Place cubes in egg mixture and lightly coat with egg and then into bread crumbs. Make sure cubes are coated completely. Refrigerate for 1 hour before cooking.

To cook croutons:

In a heavy saucepan, heat 1 cup of canola oil. Test oil to make sure it is hot enough by trying one crouton. It should start to cook immediately and turn a light brown color. Drain cooked croutons on paper towels. Serve immediately.

Tarragon Vinaigrette:

⅓   cup white wine vinegar

½   bunch fresh tarragon

1   garlic clove, peeled

½   cup extra virgin olive oil

½   cup canola oil

**   Salt and pepper to taste**

Combine vinegar, tarragon, and garlic in a blender. With the machine running, slowly drizzle in the oil until mixed. Serve on salad greens with Gorgonzola Croutons.

Serves: 6; Calories: 180; Protein: 7 g; Carbohydrate: 12 g; Total fat: 13 g;
Saturated fat: 4.5 g; Cholesterol: 50 mg; Fiber: 2 g; Sodium: 330 mg

Ginger Fruit Salad

¼   **cup honey**

1   **tablespoon lime juice**

¼   **teaspoon ground ginger**

1   **medium cantaloupe melon, peeled and cubed**

1   **medium honeydew melon, peeled and cubed**

1   **pineapple, peeled and cubed**

1   **pint raspberries or blueberries**

Mix honey, lime juice, and ginger together. Combine all diced fruit and berries in large serving bowl. Pour honey mixture over fruit and toss gently until fruit is lightly coated. Serve in small bowls with mint leaves for garnish.

Serves: 10; Calories: 120; Protein: 2 g; Carbohydrate: 31 g; Total fat: 0 g;
Saturated fat: 0 g; Cholesterol: 0 mg; Fiber: 2 g; Sodium: 45 mg

OSU's Food Science Club won first place in the 2005 NASA Food Technology Commercial Space Center Product Development Competition. Students developed the winning entry called Nutraffin, a bite-sized carrot muffin snack. The muffin received international attention.

Mixed Green Salad with Sesame Soy Dressing

2	tablespoons olive oil
1	tablespoon sesame seeds
6	tablespoons light soy sauce
½	cup canola oil
1	garlic clove
6	tablespoons red wine vinegar
½	teaspoon honey
1½	teaspoons tarragon
¾	teaspoon dried basil
½	cup light sour cream

Heat olive oil in a skillet over medium heat and add sesame seeds; cook until seeds are a light brown. This will happen quickly. Combine the rest of the ingredients into a kitchen blender. Add the sesame seeds and oil. Blend until smooth. Serve over salad greens.

Calories per tablespoon: 60; Protein: 0 g; Carbohydrate: 1 g; Total fat: 6.5 g;
Saturated fat: 1 g; Cholesterol: 3 mg; Fiber: 0 g; Sodium: 235 mg

Salad Greens with Garlic Vinaigrette

1 ½   teaspoons Dijon mustard
¼   cup red wine vinegar or balsamic vinegar
½   cup extra-virgin olive oil
¼   teaspoon freshly ground pepper
        Salt to taste
1   garlic clove, broken or crushed

Combine mustard and vinegar in a small bowl. Add olive oil in a thin stream, whisking while pouring. Season with pepper, salt if desired, and add the garlic clove. Mix to blend. For best flavor, leave dressing in refrigerator for 30 minutes to 1 hour. Dressing keeps well in the refrigerator for up to 1 week. Serve over salad greens.

Yield: 10 tablespoons; Calories: 100; Protein: 0 g; Carbohydrate: 0 g; Total fat: 11 g; Saturated fat: 1.5 g; Cholesterol: 0 mg; Fiber: 0 g; Sodium: 8.5 mg

Extra-virgin olive oil is the first cold press of the olive.

Southern-Style Salad with Spiced Pecans

Spiced Pecans:

1½	teaspoons butter
2	tablespoons honey
½	teaspoon kosher salt
½	teaspoon cayenne pepper
¼	pound (4 ounces) pecan halves

For the pecans, preheat the oven to 300°. Melt butter. Add honey, salt, and cayenne, bring to a boil, and cook 1 minute, stirring. Remove from heat, and add pecans. Stir to mix well. Spread coated pecans on a sheet pan, and bake in the oven for 10 to 12 minutes, stirring every few minutes. Take care not to burn the pecans. Serve when cooled, and store in an airtight container.

Salad Dressing:

¼	cup orange juice, preferably fresh squeezed
3	tablespoons red wine vinegar
1	tablespoon country-style Dijon mustard
2	tablespoons canola oil or light olive oil
¼	teaspoon orange zest
⅛	teaspoon ground cumin
	Fresh ground pepper and salt to taste

Whisk all ingredients together in a small bowl. Put mixed salad greens in a large bowl; pour dressing over greens and toss with Spiced Pecans.

Serves: 6; Calories: 220; Protein: 3 g; Carbohydrate: 12 g; Total fat: 19 g;
Saturated fat: 2 g; Cholesterol: 5 g; Fiber: 2 g; Sodium: 270 mg

Spinach Salad with Mandarin Oranges and Poppy Seed Dressing

5   **ounces fresh, baby spinach (or mixed salad greens)**

2   **(11 ounce) cans Mandarin oranges, drained**

⅓   **cup sliced almonds**

Rinse and dry spinach leaves. Place in bowl and toss with Mandarin orange slices. If not served immediately, cover and refrigerate. Just before serving, toss with poppy seed dressing (amount according to taste) and top with sliced almonds.

Poppy Seed Dressing:

¾   **cup sugar**

1   **teaspoon dry mustard**

½   **teaspoon salt**

⅓   **cup white vinegar**

1½   **tablespoons fresh onion juice**

1   **cup canola or safflower oil**

1½   **tablespoons poppy seeds**

In an electric blender, mix sugar, mustard, salt, vinegar, and onion juice. For the onion juice, finely chop white onion in an electric blender; put it in a fine wire mesh strainer then press to get juice. Slowly add oil, constantly blending until thick. Add poppy seeds and blend for another minute or two.

Yield: 1½ cups; Serving size: 2 tablespoons; Serves: 6; Calories: 275; Protein: 4 g;
Carbohydrate: 19 g; Total fat: 21 g; Saturated fat: 1.5 g; Cholesterol: 0 mg;
Fiber: 2.5 g; Sodium: 200 mg

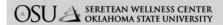

Thai Cucumber Salad

1	large cucumber, peeled, seeded and chopped
3	tablespoons red onion, finely chopped
½	cup white vinegar
¼	cup brown sugar
¼	teaspoon salt
	Black pepper to taste
	Unsalted peanuts, roasted and chopped for garnish

Combine first 6 ingredients and mix well. Chill until ready to serve. Sprinkle with chopped peanuts.

Serves: 4; Calories: 80; Protein: 1 g; Carbohydrate: 16 g; Total fat: 1.5 g;
Saturated fat: 0 g; Cholesterol: 0 mg; Fiber: 1 g; Sodium: 160 mg

Oklahoma State's latest campaign for athletic facilities is the largest single campaign in OSU history. The Next Level represents the complete renovation and reinvention of OSU's football stadium into one of the best facilities in the country. The new stadium is sure to be a source of pride for OSU fans, coaches and student-athletes.

White Bean Salad

2	(14 ounce) cans cannelloni (white beans), drained and rinsed
½	red onion, finely minced
¼	cup Italian parsley, chopped
½	red bell pepper, finely diced
½	yellow bell pepper, finely diced
⅔	cup olive oil
⅓	cup red wine vinegar
1	tablespoon fresh lemon juice
1	garlic clove, minced
	Pepper and salt to taste
	Assorted leafy greens

In medium bowl, toss together beans, onion, parsley, and peppers. In small bowl, whisk together olive oil, vinegar, lemon juice, garlic, salt and pepper. Pour 4 tablespoons of dressing onto bean mixture, and mix lightly. Set aside or refrigerate until ready to serve. Combine the mixed salad greens in a large bowl. Pour about ⅓ cup of the dressing over the salad and toss thoroughly. Leftover dressing can be stored in the refrigerator. Divide the salad evenly among 6 serving plates. Divide the cannelloni beans among the plates and grind a little fresh pepper over each salad.

Serves: 6; Calories: 250; Protein: 11 g; Carbohydrate: 32 g; Total fat: 10 g; Saturated fat: 1 g; Cholesterol: 0 mg; Fiber: 10 g; Sodium: 12 mg

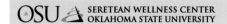
Artichokes with Lemon Vinaigrette

4	fresh artichokes
½	cup olive oil
3	tablespoons fresh lemon juice
½	teaspoon lemon zest
1	tablespoon shallot, minced
1½	teaspoons Dijon mustard
½	teaspoon sugar
	Salt and pepper to taste

Place steamer rack in large pot and fill with enough water to come just to bottom of rack. Bring to a boil. To prepare artichokes, cut off stems and remove about 1-inch off the top.

Remove any stray leaves from the bottom. Using scissors, cut off pointed tips of leaves, about ½-inch.

Arrange artichokes on rack and cover pot. Steam over medium high heat until knife pierces the base (heart) easily, adding more water if necessary, about 45 minutes.

While artichokes are steaming, prepare the vinaigrette by whisking all of the ingredients together in a bowl. Vinaigrette can be chilled or served room temperature; serve on the side as a dip for the leaves.

Serves: 8; Calories: 190; Protein: 4 g; Carbohydrate: 14 g; Total fat: 14 g; Saturated fat: 2 g; Cholesterol: 0 mg; Fiber: 7 g; Sodium: 140 mg

A diet high in vegetables and fruits can help lower blood pressure.

Braised Greens

1	tablespoon olive oil
1	bunch Russian kale, escarole or curly endive, washed and trimmed
5	garlic cloves, peeled and chopped
1	tablespoon pine nuts
1	tablespoon golden raisins
1	tablespoon chopped Kalamata olives
¼	cup water

In a large sauté pan, heat olive oil. Add the garlic and sauté for a minute. Quickly add the greens, give them a good toss. Then add the pine nuts, raisins, olives, and water. Braise until soft.

Serves: 4; Calories: 90; Protein: 3 g; Carbohydrate: 8 g; Total fat: 6 g;
Saturated fat: 1 g; Cholesterol: 0 mg; Fiber: 4 g; Sodium: 120 mg

Cauliflower Purée

2	pounds cauliflower (about 1 large head)
1	garlic clove, smashed
2	tablespoons butter
1	tablespoon olive oil
4	tablespoons low-fat milk
	Salt and pepper to taste

Bring a pot of water with steamer to boil. Cut the large core from the cauliflower and break the head into smaller sections. Place cauliflower and garlic in steamer and cook with lid until tender, about 10 minutes.

Place cauliflower, garlic, butter, olive oil, and milk in food processor or blender and purée until smooth. Season with salt and pepper.

Serves: 8; Calories: 60; Protein: 1 g; Carbohydrate: 4 g; Total fat: 4.5 g;
Saturated fat: 2 g; Cholesterol: 10 mg; Fiber: 1 g; Sodium: 20 mg

Butternut Squash Cakes

In a cuisinart with the grating attachment, grate together:

1   pound butternut squash, peeled and seeded

½   yellow onion

8   garlic cloves, peeled

In a large mixing bowl, combine the above ingredients with:

½   bunch of kale, chopped

1   whole egg

¼   cup milk

½   cup all-purpose flour

1   teaspoon baking powder

1   tablespoon mild Indian curry paste

    Pinch of salt

    Olive oil

Mix all the ingredients together. Form the mixture into small cakes (about 2 ounces). Cook the squash cakes as you would a pancake using a small amount of oil.

Serves: 8; Calories: 90; Protein: 3 g; Carbohydrate: 16 g; Total fat: 2.5 g;
Saturated fat: 0 g; Cholesterol: 25 mg; Fiber: 3 g; Sodium: 370 mg

---

**Lutein and zeaxanthin are two carotenoids that contribute the yellow color
in some fruits and vegetables, and may protect against age-related eye disease.*

Summer Squash Tart

2	medium zucchini
2	medium yellow squash
	Coarse salt and freshly ground pepper
1	tablespoon olive oil
2	large leeks, white parts only, cut into ⅓-inch dice
½	cup grated low-fat Swiss cheese (2 ounces)
1	large whole egg
1	large egg yolk
2	tablespoons evaporated skim milk
2	tablespoons heavy cream

Using a mandoline or vegetable peeler, very thinly slice 1 zucchini and 1 yellow squash lengthwise. Place slices in a colander in a single layer, and sprinkle lightly with salt. Place colander in a bowl, and set aside to drain for 30 minutes.

Cut the remaining zucchini and squash into ⅓-inch dice. In a large skillet, heat oil over high heat. Add leeks and diced squash, and season with salt and pepper. Cook until golden brown but still firm, about 8 minutes. Evenly distribute cooked vegetables in a 8-inch pie pan or an 8 x 8-inch square pan sprayed with vegetable oil. Sprinkle with grated cheese.

Place salted squash slices between double layers of paper towels. Gently press down to remove as much liquid as possible. Alternating squash colors, weave a lattice pattern over the top of the cheese and vegetables, covering the entire surface.

In a medium bowl, whisk together egg, egg yolk, evaporated skim milk, cream, and season with salt and pepper. Pour egg mixture over vegetables. Bake loosely covered with aluminum foil, until the custard is set, 30 to 35 minutes. Remove from the oven and let cool slightly before serving.

Serves: 6; Calories: 120; Protein: 5 g; Carbohydrate: 9 g; Total fat: 7 g;
Saturated fat: 2.5 g; Cholesterol: 80 mg; Fiber: 2 g; Sodium: 135 mg

---

Braised Red Cabbage
(German Style)

Day 1:

2	tablespoons sugar
1	teaspoon salt
½	teaspoon caraway seeds (or ground)
2	oranges, juiced
1	teaspoon lemon juice
1	teaspoon apple cider vinegar
1	apple, peeled, grated
1	pound red cabbage, julienne

Day 2:

2	tablespoons oil
2	tablespoons butter
½	cup chopped onions
1½	tablespoons sugar
¼	cup apple juice
¼	cup apple cider vinegar
¼	cup red wine
	Salt and pepper

On day one, in a medium-sized, glass bowl, combine all ingredients, sugar, salt, caraway seeds, orange juice, lemon juice, apple cider vinegar, and grated apple. Stir in the red cabbage and marinate overnight in the refrigerator.

On day two, in a sauté pan, heat oil and butter. Add the onions and cook until glossy. Add the sugar and stir. Cook, stirring often and watching carefully, until the sugar is caramelized, about 15 to 20 minutes. The mixture will be golden. Deglaze with apple juice, apple cider vinegar, and wine. Season with salt and pepper. Add the cabbage mixture (with the marinade) and cook, stirring occasionally, for 30 to 40 minutes until tender. Cover and keep warm until serving.

Serves: 6; Calories: 130; Protein: 1 g; Carbohydrate: 16 g; Total fat: 7 g;
Saturated fat: 2.5 g; Cholesterol: 10 mg; Fiber: 2 g; Sodium: 300 mg

Italian-Style Zucchini

2	pounds zucchini, sliced
1	tablespoon olive oil
5	garlic cloves, minced
4	tomatoes (2 pounds), peeled, seeded and quartered
¼	teaspoon salt
	Freshly ground pepper
¼	cup Parmesan cheese, freshly grated

Toss sliced zucchini with a little salt and place in a colander to drain. Heat a 10-inch skillet, add olive oil and sauté garlic for 1 minute. Add tomato and continue to cook for 10 to 15 minutes. Season with salt and pepper. Add zucchini, cover, and simmer until tender, about 10 to 20 minutes. Before serving sprinkle with Parmesan cheese.

Serves: 8; Calories: 67; Protein: 3.5 g; Carbohydrate: 9 g; Total fat: 3 g; Saturated fat: 1 g; Cholesterol: 8 mg; Sodium: 170 mg; Fiber: 1.5 g

Never refrigerate fresh tomatoes. One of the critical flavor components disappears when tomatoes are stored in the refrigerator.

Roasted Asparagus and Peppers

1	pound fresh asparagus, sliced on the diagonal
1	red bell pepper cut into 2-inch slices
1	yellow bell pepper cut into 2-inch slices
2	teaspoons olive oil

Optional dressing:

1	tablespoon balsamic vinegar
1	teaspoon maple syrup
1	tablespoon olive oil
1	teaspoon Dijon mustard
	Salt and pepper to taste

Preheat oven to 425°. On heavy sheet pan, spread vegetables out and drizzle with 2 teaspoons olive oil. Roast for 7 to 12 minutes or until crisp tender, tossing with spatula once or twice during cooking.

Whisk together the olive oil, balsamic vinegar, maple syrup, mustard, salt, and pepper. Pour over hot or room temperature vegetables.

Serves: 6; Calories: 60; Protein: 2.5 g; Carbohydrate: 4 g; Total fat: 4 g;
Saturated fat: 0 g; Cholesterol: 0 mg; Fiber: 2 g; Sodium: 20 mg

---

*Zucchini, eggplant, onions, and potatoes roast well.
Cooking time may vary, especially for potatoes.
Roasted vegetables can be added to tomato sauce or pasta.

Roasted Root Vegetables

1	small rutabaga, peeled and diced
1	parsnip, peeled and diced
1	medium turnip, peeled and diced
1-2	beets, peeled and diced
1	Yukon Gold potato, peeled and diced
2	tablespoons olive oil
1	teaspoon sea salt
8	whole cloves garlic, peeled
2	sprigs rosemary, cleaned and stemmed

Toss all vegetables in the olive oil (toss beets separately so they won't discolor the rest of the vegetables); lay vegetables in one layer on a sheet pan. Lightly salt. Bake at 400° for about 15 to 20 minutes. Once all the vegetables are almost browned, add the garlic and rosemary. Cook for 10 more minutes or until garlic is roasted. You want to add the garlic and rosemary last because they don't take as long to cook, and tend to burn easily.

Serves: 6; Calories: 130; Protein: 2 g; Carbohydrate: 20 g; Total fat: 5 g; Saturated fat: 0.5 g; Cholesterol: 0 mg; Fiber: 4 g; Sodium: 430 mg

The Coaches vs. Cancer program unites the American Cancer Society and the National Association of Basketball Coaches (NABC) in the fight against cancer. With over $140,000 raised in the 2004-2005 season, the OSU Coaches vs Cancer program ranked in the top 5 nationally. Money raised is used to benefit the Society's efforts in cancer research, advocacy, education, and patient services. To make your pledge, please contact the American Cancer Society at 1-800-ACS-2345 or visit www.osucoachesvscancer.com.

Eddie Sutton, Head Coach of OSU Men's Basketball.

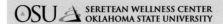

Sautéed Spinach

1   tablespoon olive oil

1   (16 ounce) bag of fresh spinach

2   teaspoons minced fresh garlic

     Salt and pepper to taste

Heat a large sauté pan over medium high heat until quite hot. Add oil and immediately add spinach and quickly toss until it begins to wilt. You may have to add a bit of water to prevent burning. Add garlic (don't let it burn!), salt and pepper and keep tossing until spinach is completely wilted. It will cook very quickly.

Serves: 4; Calories: 60; Protein: 3 g; Carbohydrate: 4 g; Total fat: 4 g; Saturated fat: 0 g; Cholesterol: 0 mg; Fiber: 3 g; Sodium: 90 mg

Spinach contains a significant source of magnesium, a mineral that helps protect bone mineral density, lowers blood pressure, and promotes heart health.

Sesame Broccoli Stir-Fry

½   **pound broccoli florets (tops of one bunch)**

2   **teaspoons oil**

2   **quarter-sized slices peeled ginger**

¼   **teaspoon salt**

¼   **teaspoon sugar**

½   **cup chicken broth or water**

2   **teaspoons sesame oil**

Break off florets and peel the skin from their small stems as much as possible. Rinse and drain florets well. Do not use the stems. Heat a wok or large, heavy skillet over high heat until hot; add the oil, swirl, and heat for 30 seconds. Toss in the ginger slices and press them in the oil; then add the broccoli and stir and toss for 5 seconds. Turn heat to medium-high and toss and turn the florets very quickly until they turn a brilliant green. Add the salt and sugar and stir briefly. Add the stock or water, cover, and steam-cook vigorously over medium-high heat for 2½ minutes. Uncover, stir the broccoli rapidly until all liquid is gone. Drizzle in the sesame oil, stir briskly for a few seconds.

Serves: 4; Calories: 95; Protein: 6.8 g; Carbohydrate: 12 g; Total fat: 4 g;
Saturated fat: 0.6 g; Cholesterol: 0; Fiber: 7 g; Sodium: 210 mg

Adding lemon juice to green vegetables causes them to change to a dull green. Try adding grated lemon zest instead. If a high-acid juice is used (lemon or orange), add it to the vegetables close to serving time.

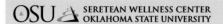

Ida's Eggplant Parmesan

	Olive oil spray
6	**large eggs**
2	**medium eggplants**
2	**cups plain bread crumbs**
1	**teaspoon dried parsley flakes or Italian seasoning**
8	**ounces part skim mozzarella cheese, sliced thin**
½	**cup (4 ounces) part skim ricotta cheese**
1	**cup (4 ounces) grated cheese (Pecorino Romano)**
	Italian Tomato Sauce, page 138

Preheat broiler. Whisk 2 eggs in a shallow bowl or plate. Pour about ½ cup bread crumbs into another plate. Lightly spray a baking sheet with olive oil spray.

Sliced the ends off the eggplant. Leaving the skin on, cut into ¼-inch slices. Slice just a few at a time to keep the eggplant from turning brown. Using a fork, dip slices in egg, coating both sides, allowing excess to drip off. Then dip both sides in bread crumbs. Arrange on the baking sheet.

Cook about 4 inches under broiler for about 5 minutes on each side. Slices should be a dark golden brown. Be careful not to let eggplant burn. Repeat process, adding an egg or more bread crumbs. Remove clumped-up bread crumbs as you proceed. (You will end up with leftover bread crumbs.) Since the eggplant slices are broiled instead of fried, they can be used right away without draining.

Preheat oven to 350°. In a 9 x 12-inch baking pan, put a thin layer of tomato sauce, just enough to cover the bottom. Arrange eggplant slices in the bottom of the pan, covering as much of the surface as possible. Layer mozzarella slices directly on top of the eggplant, covering each slice. Using about 4 tablespoons of ricotta cheese, press cheese in the spaces between the eggplant slices using a fork. Grate about 3 tablespoons of romano cheese on top. Cover completely with a thin layer of sauce, making a level surface for the next layer.

For the second layer, arrange more eggplant slices and mozzarella cheese. Spread another thin layer of sauce. Then spread another 4 tablespoons of ricotta cheese evenly with a fork. Grate another 3 tablespoons of romano cheese. For the third and top layer, arrange eggplant slices, top with remaining mozzarella cheese and remaining romano cheese. Spread sauce over top, filling in major gaps (there's no ricotta cheese on the top). Cover with aluminum foil and cook for 30 minutes. Remove foil for last 5 minutes. Dish should be bubbling around the edges. (If it is prepared ahead of time and stored in the refrigerator, cook about 15 minutes longer.) Serve with pasta or as a sandwich on Italian or French bread. This dish is even better the second day.

Serves: 12; Calories: 230; Protein: 15 g; Carbohydrate: 20 g; Total fat: 10 g;
Saturated fat: 5 g; Cholesterol: 130 mg; Fiber: 4 g; Sodium: 410 mg

VEGETABLES AND BEANS

Barbecue Baked Beans

3½   cups (1 pound, 7 ounces) dried great Northern white beans
2½   teaspoons salt
2   cups finely chopped onion
1¼   cups tomato-based mesquite or hickory-smoked barbecue sauce
10   ounces tomato-based mild or medium salsa
½   cup firmly packed golden brown sugar
¼   cup Dijon mustard
¼   cup light molasses
      Optional: ½ to 1 chipotle pepper (smoked jalapeño), canned

Rinse beans and pick through for small stones. Place beans in heavy ovenproof pan. Cover beans with cold water. Bring to a boil over medium-high heat. Remove from heat and let beans stand until cool, about 1 hour.

Drain beans and return to same pot. Cover beans generously with cold water and bring to boil over medium-high heat. Reduce heat to low and simmer bean mixture 20 minutes. Add 2 teaspoons salt and simmer until beans are tender, stirring occasionally, about 20 minutes longer. Drain beans, reserving 1½ cups bean cooking liquid.

Position rack in center of oven and preheat to 350 degrees. Combine cooked beans, reserved 1½ cups bean cooking liquid, onion, barbecue sauce, salsa, sugar, mustard, molasses, and remaining ½ teaspoon salt in same large pot.

Cover pot and bake bean mixture 1 hour. Uncover and bake until beans are very thick, stirring occasionally, about 40 minutes longer.

Serves: 12; Calories: 270; Protein: 18 g; Carbohydrate: 50 g; Total fat: 1.5 g;
Saturated fat: 0 g; Fiber: 13 gm

Beans are an excellent source of soluble fiber, helpful for lowering cholesterol.

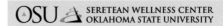

Black Beans and Rice

For the beans:

A little planning ahead is necessary to reduce the cooking time. Soak the beans overnight or for at least 8 hours.

2	**cups black turtle beans, rinsed and soaked**
8	**cups cold water**
1	**teaspoon sea salt**
1	**bay leaf**
1	**medium onion, diced**
4	**cloves garlic, smashed**

In a large pot add the above ingredients and bring up to a boil. Turn down the heat, and skim the top. Reduce heat to a slow relaxing simmer. Cook until tender about 2 hours at the most. The beans can be cooked a day ahead and reheat to serve. Garnish with 1 tablespoon of queso bianco or queso fresco cheese.

Rice:

1	**tablespoon light olive oil**
½	**medium onion, diced**
2	**cloves garlic, chopped**
3	**cups brown rice**
1	**poblano pepper, roasted, peeled and diced**
3	**cups chicken or vegetable stock**
3	**cups water**
½	**bunch cilantro, chopped fine**
1	**teaspoon sea salt**

Sauté the onions and garlic in the olive oil until golden, add rice and sauté a few more minutes. Add stock, water, pepper, cilantro, and sea salt. Bring to a boil. Stir scrapping the bottom making sure no rice is sticking. Cover with lid, turn heat down to low and let steam for about 45 minutes. When rice is done, mix well with a fork and serve.

Serves: 12; Calories: 310; Protein: 12 g; Carbohydrate: 63 g; Total fat: 2 g; Saturated fat: 0 g; Cholesterol: 0 mg; Fiber: 8 g; Sodium: 400 mg

Masoor Dal
(Red Lentils)

5   cups cold water

1½   cups red (orange) lentils

1   teaspoon salt

1   teaspoon turmeric, divided

3   large black cardamom pods, bruised

1   small stick cinnamon

3   cloves garlic, peeled and sliced

½   small onion, sliced thin

½   teaspoon coriander powder

½   teaspoon ginger powder

½   teaspoon chili powder

1   teaspoon paprika

½   small tomato, chopped

2   tablespoons oil (canola)

Place water, garlic, cinnamon stick, cardamom, salt, ½ teaspoon turmeric, and lentils in a pot and bring to a boil. Simmer 15 minutes. Cover and set aside. In a small skillet, heat the oil and fry onion until brown and crisp. Add ½ teaspoon turmeric, coriander, ginger, chili powder, and paprika. Sauté for a minute, then add the chopped tomato. Stir, adding a little water to make a paste the consistency of heavy cream. Add this mixture to the lentils. Stir well. Check the salt to taste and bring back to boil and serve over rice.

Serves: 6; Calories: 215; Protein: 14 g; Carbohydrate: 30 g; Total fat: 5 g; Saturated fat: 0 g; Cholesterol: 0; Fiber: 15 g; Sodium: 790 mg

Green vegetables (with chlorophyll) discolor when cooked or heated longer than 7 minutes. Cut vegetables small enough to cook in 6 minutes.

Vegetable Couscous Pilaf

Brown Rice Casserole

1½	tablespoons olive oil
1	large onion, chopped
2	medium carrots, diced
2	stalks celery, diced
1	red or yellow bell pepper, diced
2	medium zucchini, diced
8	ounces white mushrooms, quartered
4	cloves garlic, minced
½	teaspoon ground cumin
½	teaspoon salt
½	cup vegetable stock
4	cups cooked brown rice (1⅓ cups raw)
6	ounces low-fat Cheddar cheese, shredded
⅓	cup Parmesan cheese, grated
	Fresh herbs: parsley, thyme, or marjoram
	Optional: 8 ounces firm tofu, diced

Heat the oil in a large skillet, and sauté the onion over medium heat about 5 minutes. Add the garlic, cumin, and salt. Stir until blended and cook for 1 minute; then add the carrots, celery, and bell pepper. Cook the vegetables for about 5 minutes. Then add the zucchini and the mushrooms and cook for 7 to 10 minutes. If the pan gets too dry while vegetables are cooking, add a little of the stock.

Preheat the oven to 350°. Combine the vegetables, rice, and Cheddar cheese. Season rice mixture with a bit of salt, freshly ground black pepper, and herbs. Spoon mixture into a lightly oiled casserole dish and pour the vegetable stock over it to moisten. Top with the Parmesan cheese and cover with foil. Bake for 30 minutes. Remove foil and bake for an additional 15 minutes. Garnish with fresh parsley.

Serves: 6; Calories: 270; Carbohydrate: 39 g; Protein: 13 g; Total fat: 7 g;
Saturated fat: 2.5 g; Cholesterol: 10 mg; Fiber: 4 g; Sodium: 290 mg

Brown rice is a whole grain that can lower cholesterol, is high in fiber, and can help with weight control.

Posole (Corn Stew)

8	ounces dried posole, white or blue
½	cup finely diced onion
2	garlic cloves, minced
½	cup roasted green chiles (Anaheim or New Mexico)
2	tablespoons vegetable oil
½	teaspoon cumin powder
1	teaspoon dried oregano
2	cups low-sodium chicken broth
4-6	cups water
½	teaspoon salt or more to taste

Put posole in a large bowl and cover with water. Soak overnight, drain, and rinse the posole. This step will reduce the cooking time in half. Heat the oil in a large pot. Sauté the onion and garlic until softened. Add the cumin and oregano and stir briefly. Add the posole, green chiles, chicken broth, water, and salt. Simmer partially covered for about two hours or until the kernels have opened up and are tender. Add water as needed to keep the posole just covered with liquid. Stir the stew occasionally while cooking. Serve with Red Chile Sauce, page 139, if desired.

Serves: 10; Calories: 115; Protein: 4 g; Carbohydrate: 23 g; Total fat: 3 g;
Saturated fat: 0 g; Cholesterol: 0 mg; Fiber: 4 g; Sodium: 125 mg

Santa Fe Breakfast Casserole

2   teaspoons vegetable oil

1   onion, diced

3   medium potatoes, 1 pound, quartered, thinly sliced (Yukon Gold, red, or white potatoes)

5   large eggs

7   large egg whites

2   cups (1 pint) 1% or 2% cottage cheese, small curd

4   ounces (1¼ cups) low-fat Cheddar or Monterey Jack cheese, grated

¾   cup grated Parmesan cheese

2   (4 ounce) cans chopped green chiles, drained

⅓   cup all-purpose flour

1   teaspoon baking powder

½   teaspoon salt (optional)

Preheat oven to 350°. Lightly coat a 9 x 13-inch baking dish with nonstick cooking spray. Put oil in a large nonstick skillet over medium heat, add onions and sauté for 5 to 10 minutes. Add the potatoes to the onions and sauté until tender and browned, 10 to 15 minutes. Let cool slightly.

In a large bowl, whisk together eggs and egg whites. Add cottage, Cheddar or Monterey Jack, and Parmesan cheeses, chiles, flour, baking powder, and salt and mix thoroughly. Gently stir in the cooked potatoes. Pour into the prepared dish. Bake for 30 minutes or until lightly golden on the top and set in the center. Serve with salsa if desired.

*For a spicy dish, add 1 to 2 jalapeño peppers or for a smoky flavor add 1 to 2 chiles in adobe sauce (these peppers are found in cans in the Mexican specialty food section).

*Roasted and peeled New Mexico green chiles can be substituted for the canned chiles.

Serves: 8; Calories: 235; Protein: 21 g; Carbohydrate: 19 g; Total fat: 7 g;
Saturated fat: 3 g; Cholesterol: 145 mg; Fiber: 2 g; Sodium: 730 mg

Scallion Polenta

1	cup polenta (corn grits)
4	cups chicken stock, homemade or low-sodium
3	tablespoons fresh grated Parmesan cheese
¼	cup scallion oil
	Salt and pepper to taste

In a 2-quart saucepan, bring chicken stock to a boil. Reduce heat and gradually pour polenta into stock while whisking constantly. Whisk until any lumps are removed, and then simmer gently for 30 minutes, stirring frequently with a wooden spoon to prevent sticking.

Remove from heat and stir in Parmesan, scallion oil, and salt and pepper to taste.

For the scallion oil: (you won't need all of this for the recipe)

3	scallions, root ends removed
½	cup olive oil

Blanch scallions in boiling water for about 30 seconds until bright green; drain and cut scallions into small 1-inch pieces. Combine oil and scallions in blender and process until smooth. Scallion oil will keep in the refrigerator for about one week.

Serves: 8; Calories: 170; Protein: 4 g; Carbohydrate: 19 g; Total fat: 8 g;
Saturated fat: 1.5 g; Cholesterol: 5 mg; Fiber: 2 g; Sodium: 90 mg

Recently announced gifts totaling $2 million from ConocoPhillips will benefit more than 30 campus units. A long-time proponent of higher education, ConocoPhillips has given more than $21 million to OSU and remains the university's largest corporate donor.

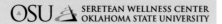
Tabbouleh

½   cup (3 ounces) fine cracked wheat

2   bunches parsley, chopped

½   bunch mint, chopped (optional)

2   large tomatoes, chopped

1   bunch green onions, finely chopped

½   large yellow onion, finely chopped

¼   cup fresh lemon juice

½   teaspoon black pepper

½   teaspoon salt

2   tablespoons canola or olive oil

Rinse cracked wheat well, then place in a large bowl and cover with water. Refrigerate while preparing vegetables. After preparing the vegetables, remove cracked wheat from refrigerator, rinse, and squeeze excess water from the wheat. Add the rest of the ingredients and season to taste.

Serves: 8; Calories: 80; Protein: 2 g; Carbohydrate: 10 g; Total fat: 4 g;
Saturated fat: 0 g; Cholesterol: 0 mg; Fiber: 2 g; Sodium: 160 mg

Vegetable Couscous Pilaf

1	tablespoon olive oil
6	green onions, thinly sliced
3	garlic cloves, minced
1	red bell pepper, seeded and diced
¼	pound snow peas
¾	cup golden raisins
3	cups low-sodium chicken stock or vegetable broth, boiling
2	tablespoons finely chopped fresh basil
2	tablespoons finely chopped fresh parsley
	Salt and pepper to taste
2	cups couscous
2	tomatoes, diced

In a large saucepan, heat the oil over medium heat. Add the green onions, garlic, red pepper, snow peas, and raisins. Sauté about 5 minutes until crisp-tender.

Pour in the boiling stock and simmer 5 minutes. Remove from the heat and add the basil, parsley, oregano, salt, and pepper to taste. Stir in the couscous. Cover and let stand 6 to 8 minutes. Add the tomatoes and gently fluff with a fork.

Serves: 6; Calories: 340; Protein: 11 g; Carbohydrate: 67 g; Total fat: 4 g;
Saturated fat: 0 g; Cholesterol: 2 mg; Fiber: 5.5 g; Sodium: 68 mg

---

OSU's architecture students have won more national and international competitions than any school in the nation except the University of Illinois.

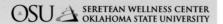

Wild Rice Pilaf

4	cups water
⅔	cup wild rice
2	tablespoons unsalted butter or olive oil
⅓	cup finely chopped carrots
⅓	cup finely chopped green onions
1	cup raw brown rice
2½	cups chicken broth
1	bay leaf
½	teaspoon dried thyme
½	teaspoon salt or to taste
	Freshly ground pepper

Combine 4 cups water in medium saucepan over high heat. Bring to a boil. Stir in wild rice. Reduce heat to low and simmer 30 minutes, stirring occasionally. Drain well.

Meanwhile, melt butter or heat oil in a large heavy casserole over medium heat. Add the carrots and green onions and sauté, stirring constantly, 4 to 5 minutes. Add the wild rice and the brown rice and stir briefly. When you are ready to bake the pilaf, preheat oven to 350°. Add the broth, bay leaf, thyme, salt and pepper to the rice. Bring the mixture to a simmer on top of the stove, then cover it tightly and transfer it to the oven.

Bake the pilaf until all the liquid has been absorbed and the rice is tender, about 50 minutes.

Serves: 8; Calories: 165; Protein: 4 g; Carbohydrate: 29 g; Total fat: 3.5 g;
Saturated fat: 2 g; Cholesterol: 8 mg; Fiber: 3 g; Sodium: 170 mg

Garlic Mashed Potatoes

2	pounds red or white potatoes, washed, peeled and cut into 3-inch pieces
4	large garlic cloves, peeled and cut into halves
1	tablespoon olive oil
1	tablespoon unsalted butter
⅓	cup low-fat milk
1	teaspoon salt or more to taste
	Fresh ground pepper to taste

Peel and dice potatoes and put in a saucepan with cold water. Let rest for 20 minutes. Pour off the water and add fresh water and bring to a boil over high heat. Add the garlic and cook until tender when pierced with a fork, about 15 minutes. Drain in a colander and return the potatoes to the pot over high heat to dry for 3 to 4 minutes.

Whip potatoes with mixer, potato masher, or food mill. Add butter, and oil; whip for a few minutes then add milk and whip until creamy. Salt and pepper to taste. Serve immediately.

Serves: 6; Calories: 150; Protein: 3 g; Carbohydrate: 25 g; Total fat: 4.5 g;
Saturated fat: 1.5 g; Cholesterol: 5 g; Fiber: 3 g; Sodium: 360 mg

Substitute 1 pound of peeled turnips for 1 pound of potatoes for a delicious and lower calorie side. Peel, dice, and cook the turnips along with the potatoes. Cooking time will be 5 to 10 minutes longer.

Grilled New Potato Salad

16	small new potatoes (1 ½ pounds) cut in half
	Olive oil for coating potatoes
	Salt and pepper to taste
¼	cup extra virgin olive oil
¼	cup fresh parsley, chopped
1	tablespoon garlic, minced
2	tablespoons fresh lemon juice
	Several dashes of Tabasco sauce
1	tablespoon whole grain Dijon mustard

Heat charcoal or gas grill. Bring large pot of water to boil. Add potatoes and cook 12 to 15 minutes, or until they can be pierced with a fork. They should be firm, but not crunchy. Drain water. Thread potatoes on skewers with cut sides facing the same way. Alternatively, spread potatoes on grill rack. Lightly spread olive oil on the potatoes, and season with salt and pepper to taste.

Grill over a medium-hot fire for 3 to 5 minutes, or until golden brown. Place cooked potatoes in a bowl. Add remaining ingredients and toss well. Serve warm or cold.

Serves: 4; Calories: 280; Protein: 5 g; Carbohydrate: 31 g; Total fat: 16 g;
Saturated fat: 2 g; Cholesterol: 0 mg; Fiber: 4 g; Sodium: 410 mg

Mashed Russet and Sweet Potatoes

1½	**pounds russet white potatoes, peeled and cut into 1-inch pieces**
1	**pound sweet potatoes, peeled and cut into 1-inch pieces**
¼	**cup buttermilk or milk**
1	**tablespoon honey**
2	**tablespoons olive oil**
1	**tablespoon butter**
	Salt and pepper to taste
	Chives or green onion tops, chopped for garnish

Simmer potatoes in boiling water until tender (about 15 minutes). Drain potatoes and place back in pan over low heat for several minutes to slightly dry. Whip potatoes with potato masher or hand mixer slowly adding buttermilk. Mix in honey, olive oil, butter, salt and pepper to taste. Serve immediately, topped with chopped chives or green onions. If potatoes must be held before serving, place in double boiler over low simmer, covered.

Serves: 6; Calories: 235; Protein: 4 g; Carbohydrate: 42 g; Total fat: 6 g; Saturated fat: 1 g; Cholesterol: 0 mg; Fiber: 4 g; Sodium: 425 mg

Sweet potatoes contain beta-carotene, a nutrient that may protect against age-related eye disease.

Roasted Herbed Red Potatoes

2   **pounds red potatoes**

1   **tablespoon olive oil**

1   **teaspoon Kosher salt**

½   **teaspoon fresh ground black pepper**

2   **tablespoons each fresh chopped herbs (parsley, rosemary, chives)**

Wash and quarter red potatoes. If potatoes are large, cut into smaller pieces. Toss in large bowl with fresh chopped herbs and just enough olive oil to coat (about 1 tablespoon). Roast in 425° oven for 20 minutes or until fork tender.

Serves: 6; Calories: 130; Protein: 3 g; Carbohydrate: 24 g; Total fat: 2.5 g; Saturated fat: 0 g; Cholesterol: 0 mg; Fiber: 3 g; Sodium: 320 mg

*Don't peel the potatoes; the skin provides extra fiber.

Stuffed Baked Potatoes

4	large baking potatoes
	Vegetable oil, for rubbing potatoes
1	cup low-fat cottage cheese
½	cup plain low-fat yogurt
1	large rib celery, finely diced
2	tablespoons chopped onion
1	cup broccoli florets
¼	pound mozzarella cheese cut into thin slices
	Pepper to taste

Preheat oven to 375°. Rub the potatoes with the oil and bake for 60 to 70 minutes until tender (or microwave potatoes until fork tender). In a medium bowl, stir together the cottage cheese, yogurt, celery, scallions, and pepper. Halve the potatoes lengthwise and scoop out the flesh, leaving a ½-inch potato shell. Stir the potato into the cottage cheese mixture.

Arrange the potato shells in a baking dish. Fill the shells with the potato-cheese filling. Top with the broccoli florets and cover with the sliced mozzarella. Bake for 15 minutes, or until the potatoes are heated and the cheese is melted. Season to taste with pepper.

Serves: 4; Calories: 365; Protein: 21 g; Carbohydrate: 58 g; Total fat: 6 g;
Saturated fat: 3.5 g; Cholesterol: 20 mg; Fiber: 6 g; Sodium: 415 mg

Potatoes are a good source of potassium.

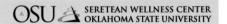
Sweet Potato Salad with Chipotle Chili

2   **pounds sweet potatoes, peeled and cut into 1-inch pieces**

⅓   **cup extra-virgin olive oil (divided)**

½   **large or 1 small red bell pepper, roasted, skinned and diced**

2   **tablespoons fresh lime juice**

½   **teaspoon chili powder**

½   **teaspoon ground cumin powder**

1   **diced chipotle chili (canned in sauce), or to taste**

¼   **cup light mayonnaise**

     Salt to taste

¼   **cup finely chopped fresh cilantro leaves**

4   **scallions, white and light green parts, finely chopped**

Lightly coat sweet potatoes with olive oil (about 2 teaspoons). Roast sweet potatoes on heavy sheet pan lined with parchment paper in 400° oven for 30 minutes or until soft. Set aside. Roast red pepper under broiler until charred on outside; put in a covered bowl or bag to cool. Skin pepper and dice.

To make dressing, whisk together olive oil, lime juice, chili powder, cumin, chipotle chili, light mayonnaise, and salt. Add red bell pepper, cilantro, and scallions to potatoes and toss with dressing. Serve warm or refrigerate and bring to room temperature before serving. It can be made a day ahead.

Serves: 6; Calories: Protein: 3 g; Carbohydrate: 43 g; Total fat: 13 g;
Saturated fat: 1.5 g; Cholesterol: 0 mg; Fiber: 5 g; Sodium: 150 mg

Roasting sweet potatoes brings out the sugar so they taste even sweeter!

Cucumber Dill Sauce

Pesto (Fresh Basil Sauce)

3   cups fresh basil leaves

3   garlic cloves

½   cup pine nuts (may substitute walnuts or pecans)

½   cup Parmesan cheese, finely grated

⅓-½ cup extra virgin olive oil

     Salt to taste

Wash basil leaves (just before using), dry, and remove large parts of stems. In a food processor, finely chop garlic, add basil and chop, and then add nuts and chop. With food processor running, slowly add ⅓ cup of olive oil, then add Parmesan cheese. Taste for salt. Add more oil or water, if desired, to thin the consistency of sauce. Purée until pesto is smooth and creamy.

Pesto may be frozen. Put in a plastic container, spread a light layer of olive oil over pesto and cover the container (keep airtight to retain light green, fresh color). It may also be kept in the refrigerator, in an airtight container, for several days.

Pesto can be stirred into drained, hot pasta for a quick, easy and healthy meal. When using pesto that has been frozen, the consistency can be thinned and smoothed by adding a few drops of warm water.

Serving size: 1 ounce; Calories: 140; Protein: 3 g; Carbohydrate: 2 g; Total fat: 14 g;
Saturated fat: 2.5 g; Cholesterol: 0 mg; Fiber: < 1 g; Sodium: 40 mg

Milton Quarterly

*A internationally respected scholarly journal, Milton Quarterly publishes work on the
seventeenth century English poet, John Milton, his career, his literary surroundings and his place in cultural history.
In 2005 Oklahoma State University became the journal's academic home.*

Cilantro Pesto

6	garlic cloves
½	cup fresh cilantro leaves
1	cup fresh parsley leaves
1	tablespoon dried oregano
¼	teaspoon salt
¼	teaspoon rice vinegar
½	cup olive oil

Mince garlic in food processor. Add the cilantro, parsley, salt and oregano. Finely chop in processor, scraping down bowl occasionally. Add the vinegar and olive oil in a steady stream to the herbs while processor is running. Season to taste with pepper. Serve with Black Bean Chili, page 28.

Serving Size: 1 tablespoon; Calories: 108; Protein: 0 g; Carbohydrate: 2 g; Total fat: 11 g; Saturated fat: 1.5 g; Cholesterol: 0 mg; Fiber: 0 g; Sodium: 115 mg

Green Salsa

8-10	small tomatillos or 3-5 large (plum size), paper shell removed
1-2	jalapeño peppers, stem and seeds removed
1-2	green onions
1	large garlic clove
2	tablespoons cilantro
	Salt to taste

Bring a pot of water to a boil and add tomatillos and peppers; boil until softened, about 15 minutes. Drain the tomatillos and peppers; put in a blender with the onions, garlic, and cilantro. Purée until desired consistency. Salt to taste. Serve with Vegetable Quesadillas, page 20.

Yield: 1-1½ cups; Calories: 70; Protein: 2 g; Carbohydrate: 14 g; Total fat: 2 g; Saturated fat: 0 g; Cholesterol: 0 mg; Fiber: 5 g; Sodium: 10 mg

Pomegranate Cucumber Mint Salsa

½ cup pine nuts

2   tablespoons mint jelly

2   tablespoons white wine vinegar

1   tablespoon olive oil

1   cucumber, peeled, seeded and cut into small dice

    Seeds from 1 large pomegranate

2   tablespoons fresh mint, chopped

1   small garlic clove, minced

    Salt and pepper to taste

Toast pine nuts in a dry pan over moderate heat until golden. In a bowl, whisk the jelly, vinegar and oil. Add remaining salsa ingredients and toss. Season with salt and pepper. Serve with cooked lamb or pork.

Yield: 2 cups; Serves: 8; Calories: 90; Protein: 2 g; Carbohydrate: 8 g; Total fat: 6 g; Saturated fat: 1 g; Cholesterol: 0 mg; Fiber: < 1 g; Sodium: 0 mg

Cucumber Dill Sauce

½ cup nonfat sour cream

½ cup lowfat sour cream

3   tablespoons fresh dill, chopped

1   tablespoon Dijon mustard

1   teaspoon fresh lemon juice

¼ cup seeded, diced cucumber

¼ teaspoon salt

In small bowl, mix together the two types of sour cream, fresh dill, mustard, lemon juice, cucumbers, and salt. Serve over grilled salmon.

Serves: 4; Calories: 80; Protein: 4 g; Carbohydrate: 8 g; Total fat: 2.5 g; Saturated fat: 2 g; Cholesterol: 15 mg; Fiber: 0 g; Sodium: 280 mg

Bulgogi Sauce

3	tablespoons light soy sauce
2	teaspoons sesame oil
2	tablespoons water
2	tablespoons rice wine vinegar
1	teaspoon toasted sesame seeds
2	teaspoons finely chopped green onion
½	teaspoon chili paste (optional)
1	garlic clove, crushed
2	teaspoons sugar
	Salt to taste

Put soy sauce and sesame oil in a small bowl and stir in the next 6 ingredients. Crush garlic with sugar and salt to make a fine paste. Stir paste into sauce and mix well. Serve in small individual sauce dishes with grilled meat.

Serves: 8; Calories: 25; Protein: 1.5 g; Carbohydrate: 2 g; Total fat: 1.5 g;
Saturated fat: 0 g; Cholesterol: 0 mg; Fiber: 0 g; Sodium: 385 mg

Firecracker Sauce

¼   red onion, roughly chopped

½   cucumber, peeled, seeded, and roughly chopped

⅓   cup cilantro

⅓   cup rice vinegar

½   cup olive oil

1   tablespoon sesame oil

1   teaspoon fresh ginger, chopped

2   garlic cloves

2   tablespoons hot bean paste (or to taste)

⅔   cup sweet chili sauce (Mae Ploy)

In a kitchen blender, purée red onion, cucumber, ginger, garlic, and cilantro. Gradually add the rice vinegar, olive oil, sesame oil and sweet chili sauce; blend mixture until smooth. Serve as a dipping sauce for crispy tofu triangles or fresh spring rolls.

Yield: 3 cups; Serves: 12 (2 ounces portions); Calories: 70; Protein: 0 g; Carbohydrate: 6 g; Total fat: 5 g; Saturated fat: .5 g; Cholesterol: 0 mg; Fiber: 0 g; Sodium: 190 mg

Red Pepper Coulis

1   **large red bell pepper**

2   **tablespoons red onion, chopped**

1   **clove garlic, chopped**

2   **teaspoons olive oil**

⅓   **cup low-sodium vegetable stock**

1   **teaspoon balsamic vinegar**

     Salt and pepper to taste

Roast the pepper under the broiler or over the flame of a gas stove, rotating once or twice, until skin is charred. Place in a closed bag for 10 to 15 minutes. While pepper is cooling, heat a small pan and add oil, onion, and garlic, sautéing briefly until onion is translucent. Be careful not to burn the garlic. Set aside.

When pepper is cool enough to handle, remove skin, stem, and seeds and rinse briefly under water. Place the pepper, onion and garlic, and chicken stock in a blender and blend until smooth, adding more stock if necessary to adjust consistency. Season with salt and pepper. Serve at room temperature, or warm it briefly.

Yield: 4 (2 ounce) servings; Calories: 30; Protein: 0 g; Carbohydrate: 2 g; Total fat: 2 g; Saturated fat: 0 g; Cholesterol: 0 mg; Fiber: < 1 g; Sodium: 5 mg

---

Pico De Gallo

2	garlic cloves, very finely chopped
1	jalapeño pepper, seeded and very finely chopped
1	poblano pepper, seeded and very finely chopped
1	New Mexico chili, roasted, peeled, seeded and very finely chopped or 2 ounces (½ small can) of chopped green chilies, finely chopped
3	medium, ripe, tomatoes, very finely chopped and drained
2	green onions, finely chopped, using most of the green
½	cup cilantro, finely chopped
½	lime, squeeze into mixture to taste
	Salt to taste

Chop the tomatoes and let them drain well. In a bowl, mix together the peppers, green onions, garlic, cilantro, and drained tomatoes. Season with salt and lime juice. Serve with tortilla chips or use on beans, chili, or tacos.

Serves: 6; Calories: 22; Protein: 0 g; Carbohydrate: 5 g; Total fat: 0 g;
Saturated fat: 0 g; Cholesterol: 0 mg; Fiber: 1.5 g; Sodium: 40 mg

Pizza Sauce

1	pound, 12 ounces tomato sauce
2	cloves chopped garlic
1	tablespoon dried oregano
1	teaspoon dried basil
1	teaspoon honey or sugar
1-2	tablespoons olive oil

Blend the above ingredients together until smooth. Refrigerate sauce until ready to assemble the pizza (this sauce is not cooked).

Calories: 35; Protein: 1 g; Carbohydrate: 5 g; Total fat: 1 g;
Saturated fat: 0 g; Cholesterol: 0 mg; Fiber: 1 g; Sodium: 160 mg

Tomato Sauce

3	(14 ounce) cans of peeled or diced unsalted tomatoes
1	tablespoon olive oil
5	cloves garlic, minced
1	tablespoon tomato paste
½	cup of fresh basil, chopped

Crush tomatoes in blender or food processor (including juice). In large skillet or saucepan, warm the olive oil over low heat. Add the garlic. Stir until the garlic begins to color (watch carefully since garlic burns easily).

Stir in tomatoes and tomato paste and bring to a simmer. Keep heat low. Simmer uncovered for 30 minutes; stir in chopped basil and simmer an additional 15 minutes.

Yield: 2 cups; Serves: 4; Calories: 100; Protein: 3 g; Carbohydrate: 15 g; Total fat: 4 g;
Saturated fat: 0 g; Cholesterol: 0 mg; Fiber: 3 g; Sodium: 65 mg

Italian Tomato Sauce

2	tablespoons extra virgin olive oil
1	medium onion, chopped (1 cup)
2	large cloves garlic, sliced
½	cup celery, finely chopped
½	cup carrot, finely chopped
¼	cup red wine (optional)
3	cups chopped canned (no salt) tomatoes, seeded
6	cups canned tomatoes (chopped and seeded)
1	cup water
1½	tablespoons dried basil (or 3 tablespoons shredded fresh basil)
1½	tablespoons dried oregano (or 3 tablespoons shredded fresh oregano leaves)
	Salt and pepper to taste

Heat oil, onion, and garlic in Dutch oven on medium heat until onion is just golden, stirring often and turning garlic slices. Be sure not to burn garlic. Add carrots and celery; stir vegetables and cook an additional 5 minutes. If using wine, add ¼ cup at this time and stir. Cook about 5 minutes. Add tomatoes, water, basil, and oregano. Cover and simmer on low for 1½ to 2 hours. Stir every 15 minutes.

Yield: 8 cups; Calories per cup: 100; Protein: 5 g; Carbohydrate: 14 g; Total fat: 3 g; Saturated fat: 0 g; Cholesterol: 0 g; Fiber: 4 g; Sodium: 215 mg

Makes enough sauce for eggplant Parmesan recipe and about 2 pounds of fresh pasta.

Fresh tomatoes can be substituted for canned when in season.

Red Chile Sauce

1	tablespoon light olive oil
2	tablespoons unbleached white flour
4	tablespoons onion, finely chopped
1	garlic clove, peeled and finely chopped
¼	teaspoon oregano
1	teaspoon powdered cumin
½	cup powdered red chilies
2½	cups water
¼	teaspoon salt

Heat oil over medium heat. Add the onion and garlic; sauté for about 5 minutes. Stir in the spices and flour and cook, stirring constantly, until mixture turns a light brown (this will take several minutes). Mix the powdered chilies and water together in a separate bowl. Pour them into the flour paste, stirring to prevent lumps. Stir until the sauce is thickened. Chilies can scorch easily so keep the heat low. This sauce can be puréed for a smoother consistency. Serve with posole or beans.

Ground red chiles or posole can be ordered by mail from many New Mexico stores. Hatch or Chimayo chiles are widely available.

Light Pan Gravy

2	tablespoons olive oil
2	tablespoons onion, minced
2	tablespoons flour
1¼	cups low-sodium chicken broth, divided
	Salt and pepper to taste

After searing meat (chicken, beef, or pork) in a hot pan, set meat aside and add olive oil to the pan; add onion and sauté briefly. Combine ¼ cup cold chicken stock with the flour; whisk until smooth and set aside.

Add remaining chicken stock to onions to deglaze the pan and loosen all the bits of browned meat; slowly whisk flour mixture into the pan and stir to desired consistency. For a thinner gravy, add more stock. Season with salt and pepper.

Serve 4; Calories: 90; Protein: 1 g; Carbohydrate: 4 g; Total fat: 7 g; Saturated fat: 1 g; Cholesterol: 0 g; Fiber: 0 g; Sodium: 180 mg

Angel Food Cake

1	cup sifted cake flour
1½	cups granulated sugar
¼	teaspoon salt
12	large egg whites
1¼	teaspoons cream of tartar
1¼	teaspoons lemon extract

Preheat oven to 375°. Stir flour with ¾ cup sugar and salt. Beat egg whites in clean dry bowl with cream of tartar until soft peaks form. Add lemon extract. Add the remaining sugar, 2 tablespoons at a time; beat well after each addition. Sift ¼ cup flour mixture over egg whites and fold in carefully with a spatula. Fold in remaining flour mixture by fourths. Turn into a 10-inch tube pan. Bake 35 to 40 minutes or until a toothpick inserted in the center comes out clean. Invert tube of pan over the neck of a bottle (or rest upside down at an angle; cool completely. Remove from pan.

Serves: 12; Calories: 145; Protein: 4 g; Carbohydrate: 33 g; Total fat: 0 g;
Saturated fat: 0 g; Cholesterol: 0 mg; Fiber: 0 g; Sodium: 105 mg

The OSU Seretean Wellness Center has twice been recognized for
helping make the university a healthier place to work and study. It's the second
consecutive year the Wellness Center has received the Oklahoma Certified Healthy Business Award,
given to businesses and workplaces that promote a healthy lifestyle. The award is given by
The Oklahoma Health Department, Oklahoma Academy for State Goals
and Oklahoma Turning Point Council Honorees.

Apple Cobbler

¼	cup sugar
1	teaspoon cinnamon
¼	teaspoon nutmeg
⅓	cup water
2	teaspoons freshly squeezed lemon juice
6	large apples (McIntosh, Jonathan, or Granny Smith)
1	(8 ounce) package light cream cheese
2	tablespoons unsalted butter
¾	cup granulated sugar
¾	cup unbleached all-purpose flour
¼	teaspoon salt

Mix ¼ cup sugar, cinnamon, and nutmeg together and set aside. Mix water and lemon juice in another bowl and set aside. Lightly butter 2 to 3 quart soufflé dish. Peel, core, and slice apples into prepared dish. Sprinkle with sugar and spice mixture. Pour water and lemon juice mixture over all. Blend cream cheese, butter, ¾ cup sugar, flour, and salt in food processor (or use pastry cutter). Spread over apples and bake in preheated 350° oven approximately 1 hour or until lightly browned and apples are soft.

Serves: 8; Calories: 285; Protein: 4 g; Carbohydrate: 50 g; Total fat: 8 g;
Saturated fat: 5 g; Cholesterol: 21 g; Fiber: 2 g; Sodium: 235 mg

Apple Nut Cake

½   cup coarsely chopped walnuts or pecans

2   cups diced peeled tart green apples (such as Granny Smith; about 2 small)

¼   cup orange juice

¾   cup sugar

¼   cup apple butter

¼   cup canola oil

1   large egg

¾   cup all-purpose flour

½   cup whole wheat pastry flour*

1   teaspoon ground cinnamon

1   teaspoon baking soda

½   teaspoon salt

Preheat oven to 350°. Spray 9 x 9-inch baking pan or round 10-inch cake pan with vegetable oil and flour lightly. Place nuts on sheet pan and put in the oven for 5 minutes or until lightly browned; set the timer—they burn easily. Pour orange juice over diced apples to keep apple from browning. Mix sugar, apple butter, oil, and egg in large bowl to blend. Stir in diced apples and orange juice. Sift flour, cinnamon, baking soda, and salt over apple mixture. Add chopped walnuts; mix thoroughly. Transfer mixture to prepared pan.

Bake until cake is light brown and crusty on top and tester inserted into center comes out clean, about 30 minutes. Cool cake in pan on rack.

Serves: 12; Calories: 200; Carbohydrate: 29 g; Protein: 3 g; Total fat: 8 g; Saturated fat: 1 g; Cholesterol: 20 mg; Fiber: 2 g; Sodium: 160 mg

*Whole wheat pastry flour can be found in most natural food stores or baking section at a grocery store.

Balsamic Berries and Apples

1	quart fresh strawberries, hulled and quartered
1	cup fresh raspberries
1	cup fresh blueberries
1	tart apple (Granny Smith) peeled and diced
¼	cup apple juice concentrate, thawed
3	tablespoons fresh orange juice
2	tablespoons Balsamic vinegar
1	orange, grated zest (orange outer rind)

Combine berries and apple in glass or non-aluminum bowl. In separate bowl, whisk together apple juice concentrate, orange juice, Balsamic vinegar, and orange zest. Pour the mixture over fruit and toss well.

Marinate fruit in refrigerator for at least 30 minutes or up to 6 hours. When ready to serve, spoon fruit over cup of light ice cream, frozen yogurt or angel food cake.

Serves: 6; Calories: 90; Protein: 1 g; Carbohydrate: 23 g; Total fat: 0 g;
Saturated fat: 0 g; Cholesterol: 0 mg; Fiber: 5 g; Sodium: 5 mg

---

*Berries are a top ten best food—they provide fiber, vitamin C, and anti-cancer substances.
Frozen berries have the same nutrients as fresh and are great in fruit smoothies.
Fresh berries are best for this recipe.*

Cherry Chocolate Biscotti

1 ½   cups all-purpose white flour

¾   teaspoon baking powder

¼   teaspoon salt

4   tablespoons unsalted butter, softened

½   cup white sugar plus 2 tablespoons

1   whole egg

1   teaspoon vanilla extract

⅔   cup dried cherries or cranberries

⅓   cup dark chocolate chips

Stir together flour, baking powder, and salt. Beat butter with electric mixer; add sugar, egg, and vanilla extract and beat well. Mix in flour. Roughly chop dried fruit and chocolate; mix into dough until blended.

Lightly flour cutting board. Shape dough into cylinder shape to form one long log. Place log on sheet pan lined with parchment paper. Refrigerate dough for about 20 minutes. Preheat oven to 350°. Bake for 25 to 30 minutes, or until firm to the touch. Let log cool on pan for 15 minutes. Place log on cutting board and slice it diagonally ½-inch thick.

Lay slices back on the sheet pan and bake for 10 to 12 minutes. Cool biscotti on rack; store in an airtight container.

Yield: 20 cookies; Calories: 100; Protein: 1 g; Carbohydrate: 18 g; Total fat: 3 g;
Saturated fat: 1.5 g; Cholesterol: 20 mg; Fiber: 0 g; Sodium: 55 mg

Chocolate contains compounds that may be beneficial to cardiovascular health-in moderation of course!

Chocolate Fudge Cake

This cake is made with a food processor.

¾	cup all-purpose flour
½	teaspoon baking powder
¼	teaspoon baking soda
¼	teaspoon salt
2	ounces unsweetened chocolate, coarsely chopped
1¼	cups sugar
1	tablespoon unsweetened cocoa powder
⅓	cup boiling water
¼	cup unsalted butter
¼	cup light olive oil
2	large eggs
½	cup light sour cream

Glaze:

2	ounces semisweet chocolate, broken into pieces
⅓	cup powdered sugar, sifted
1	tablespoon unsalted butter
2	tablespoons milk

Preheat oven to 325°. Spray a 10-inch x 2-inch high pan with Baker's Joy. Combine flour, baking powder, salt, and soda in food processor for 5 seconds; set aside. Combine chocolate, sugar, and cocoa—process for 1 minute. Add boiling water and butter-process for 1 minute. Add eggs-process 1 minute. Add light olive oil-process 30 seconds. Add sour cream-process 5 seconds. Add flour mixture to the processor and mix for a few seconds. Pour into prepared pan and bake for 45 minutes. Let cool for 5 to 10 minutes and remove from pan. Cool completely before topping with chocolate glaze.

For the glaze, heat over very low heat until smooth. Refrigerate until thickened (15 to 20 minutes). Pour over cooled cake and smooth over sides and top.

Serves: 12; Calories: 250; Protein: 3 g; Carbohydrate: 36 g; Total fat: 12 g;
Saturated fat: 4 g; Cholesterol: 35 mg; Fiber: 1 g; Sodium: 170 mg

If chocolate is heated above 120°, it will separate into cocoa butter and cocoa particles. When this happens, it is best to discard the chocolate and start the recipe over.

Cowboy Cookies

½	cup apple butter
½	cup unsalted butter, softened
1	cup brown sugar
1	cup granulated sugar
2	eggs
2	teaspoons vanilla
2¾	cups unbleached flour
1	teaspoon salt
1	teaspoon baking powder
1	teaspoon baking soda
2	cups rolled oats
1¾	cups chocolate chips
⅔	cup chopped walnuts or pecans

Preheat oven to 350°. Whip butter and sugar together gradually adding apple butter until creamy and smooth. Add eggs and vanilla and mix well. Mix flour with salt, baking powder, baking soda and oats and add to butter mixture. Stir in remaining ingredients.

Form cookies into small balls. Bake on parchment-lined baking sheets for 12 minutes or until light brown.

Yield: 30 cookies; Calories: 250; Protein: 4 g; Carbohydrate: 38 g; Total fat: 8 g; Saturated fat: 3.5 g; Cholesterol: 15 mg; Fiber: 2 g; Sodium: 150 mg

---

Parchment paper is available at most grocery stores.
Use it to prevent food from sticking when roasting vegetables or baking.

Farmer's Market Strawberry Shortcake

3	tablespoons vegetable oil
½	cup white sugar
1	teaspoon vanilla
¼	cup skim milk
¼	cup plain yogurt
1	cup cake flour
½	teaspoon baking soda
2	egg whites

Preheat oven to 350°. Spray an 8 or 9-inch cake pan with cooking oil. In a medium bowl, whisk the oil, sugar, and vanilla until well blended. Stir in the milk and yogurt. In a separate bowl, sift flour and baking soda together. Add the flour to yogurt mixture and beat well. In a dry, clean bowl, whip egg whites until stiff. Fold them into the flour mixture. Transfer batter to prepared pan; bake for 30 minutes or until the center of cake springs back to the touch. Let cool in pan for 15 minutes, then turn the cake out onto a rack and let cool.

Strawberries:

3	pints strawberries (2 pounds), hulled and quartered
2	tablespoons sugar, or to taste
½	cup cold heavy cream
2	tablespoons powdered sugar, or to taste
½	teaspoon vanilla

Gently mash strawberries with granulated sugar in a large bowl with potato masher just until berries release their juices, being careful not to crush them to a pulp. Let stand at room temperature, stirring occasionally, for 1 hour.

Beat heavy cream and confectioner's sugar in a medium bowl with an electric mixer until cream holds soft peaks. Beat in vanilla.

Split cake horizontally in half. Spoon half the strawberry mixture over top of bottom layer of cake. Place other half of cake on top; spread with remaining strawberries. Cut into 10 portions. Spoon whipped cream on each serving. Drizzle with strawberry juice.

Serves: 10; Calories: 220; Protein: 3 g; Carbohydrate: 32 g; Total fat: 9 g;
Saturated fat: 3 g; Cholesterol: 15 mg; Fiber: 2 g; Sodium: 85 mg

Lemon Orange Spice Cake

3   cups all-purpose flour

1   teaspoon baking soda

1   cup light olive oil

1   cup sugar

1   tablespoon grated orange peel

⅓   cup fresh squeezed orange juice

1   teaspoon grated lemon peel

¼   cup fresh squeezed lemon juice

¼   cup cold water

1   teaspoon ground cinnamon

1   cup red seedless grapes

1   tablespoon brandy

Butter and flour a 9-inch cake pan and set aside. Sift the flour with the baking soda. In a medium bowl beat the oil adding the sugar a little at a time. When all the sugar has been added, fold in the flour mixture with the lemon juice, orange juice, and water with grated orange and lemon peel. Mix until all is incorporated. Gently fold in grapes. Pour mixture into cake pan and bake at 350° for 45 to 50 minutes. Remove from oven and cool on rack before removing from the pan.

Grape Sauce:

3   cups red seedless grapes, cleaned

1   cup water

1   cup sugar

In a medium saucepan combine the sugar and water and bring to a boil. Simmer and reduce by one quarter. Add the grapes and continue to simmer until grapes are shiny and plump but not yet broken. Cool and serve over individual slices of cake.

Serves: 12; Calories: 400; Protein: 3 g; Carbohydrate: 66 g; Total fat: 14 g;
Saturated fat: 2 g; Cholesterol: 0 mg; Fiber: 2 g; Sodium: 105 mg

*For baking, make sure you use light olive oil.

DESSERTS

Lemon Snow Balls

5	large lemons
2	teaspoons finely grated lemon zest
¾	cup fresh lemon juice
1	cup whole milk
1	cup plain yogurt
1	cup sugar
	Fresh raspberries
	Mint leaves

Cut lemons in half lengthwise to resemble boats. Cut a small sliver of peel from bottom of lemons. With a spoon, remove pulp from lemons to form a shell. Put lemon shells in a container (do not stack). Cover with plastic wrap and freeze.

In a freezer safe bowl, combine lemon zest, lemon juice, milk, and yogurt. Add sugar and stir until dissolved. Cover with plastic wrap and freeze 8 hours or overnight. (Alternatively, put mixture in ice cream freezer and follow manufacturer's instructions.)

Remove from freezer. If necessary to break up ice crystals, process in food processor or beat with electric mixer until smooth. Do not over process. Freeze for at least 2 hours or up to 2 days. Spoon into lemon shells or spoon the mixture into the shells and then freeze. Garnish with fresh raspberries and mint.

Serves: 10; Calories: 110; Protein: 2 g; Carbohydrate: 24 g; Total fat: 1.5 g;
Saturated fat: 1 g; Cholesterol: 5 mg; Fiber: 0 g; Sodium: 25 mg

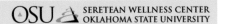

Maple-Nut Fruit Crisp

⅓   cup flour

⅓-½   cup packed light brown sugar

⅓   cup regular oats

¼   teaspoon cinnamon

¼   cup chilled unsalted butter

¼   cup chopped walnuts, pecans or almonds

7   cups sliced and peeled apples (3 pounds) Rome and McIntosh

¼   cup pure maple syrup

½   teaspoon cinnamon

Preheat oven to 350°. In a small bowl, mix flour, brown sugar, oats, cinnamon, and walnuts. Cut butter into oat mixture. In a large bowl, mix sliced apples, maple syrup, and cinnamon. Put apples in a 1½-quart baking dish (13 x 9-inch if you double the recipe). Spread oat mixture over the top and bake for 45 to 50 minutes. Bake until lightly browned on top and apples are bubbling. If the crisp browns too quickly, cover loosely with aluminum foil. Serve with light ice cream if desired.

Serves: 8; Calories: 270; Protein: 1 g; Carbohydrate: 50 g; Total Fat: 9 g;
Saturated Fat: 4 g; Cholesterol: 16 mg; Fiber: 4 g; Sodium: 7 mg

*Nuts are a natural source of Vitamin E.

*If you prefer a sweeter dessert, use ½ cup brown sugar.

Molasses Cake with Warm Apple Compote

For the cake:

1½	cups boiling water
1	cup molasses
1	teaspoon baking soda
½	cup unsalted butter, room temperature
1	cup firmly packed brown sugar
1	large egg
½	teaspoon salt
2	teaspoons ground ginger
1¼	teaspoons ground cinnamon
2½	cups all-purpose flour
1	tablespoon baking powder

Combine the molasses with the boiling water. Remove from heat, stir in the baking soda. Set aside and let cool to room temperature. Combine the dry ingredients. Cream the butter and sugar until light and fluffy. Alternately fold the cooked molasses and the dry ingredients into the mixer with the creamed butter mixture. Pour into a cake pan sprayed with Baker's Joy. Bake for 45 - 50 minutes.

For the compote:

7	apples
2	tablespoons butter
½	cup brown sugar
¼	cup brandy
½	tablespoon fresh lemon juice
	Pinch of salt

Peel, core, and dice the apples. Melt the butter in a sauce pan. Add the apples, brown sugar, brandy, lemon, and salt. Simmer until the apples become a little soft and sauce thickens slightly. Pour over each piece of cake just before serving. Garnish with frozen yogurt if desired.

Serves: 12; Calories: 410; Protein: 3 g; Carbohydrate: 75 g; Total fat: 10 g;
Saturated fat: 6 g; Cholesterol: 45 mg; Fiber: 2 g; Sodium: 360 mg

Nectarine and Berry Crisp

¾   cup plus 2 tablespoons all-purpose flour

⅓   cup brown sugar

4   teaspoons white sugar

⅛   teaspoon cinnamon

⅓   cup unsalted butter (softened)

2½   pounds nectarines, sliced (peeled optional)

1   cup raspberries

1   tablespoon all-purpose flour

½   cup white sugar

In medium bowl, mix together first 4 ingredients. Cut in butter with your fingers or pastry blender. When mixture is beginning to hold together and look crumbly, set aside and prepare fruit.

Wash nectarines, peel if desired and slice them ½-inch thick (4 to 5 cups total). Add berries, sugar, and flour; toss together lightly. Spoon into deep pie pan or gratin dish of similar size. Spread topping over fruit and bake in preheated 375° oven 35 minutes, or until the top is golden and fruit is tender. Juices will bubble thick around the edges. Serve with light ice cream if desired.

Serves: 8; Calories: 246; Protein: 3 g; Carbohydrates: 41 g; Total fat: 9 g;
Saturated fat: 3 g; Cholesterol: 0 mg; Fiber: 3 g; Sodium: 0 mg

OSU's William S. Spears School of Business Trading Floor
is one of only a few such facilities in the nation. The state-of-the-art trading floor gives
students hands-on experience in managing information to assess financial risk.